TO LIVE AND TO WRITE

TO LIVE
AND TO WRITE

Selections by Japanese Women Writers 1913-1938

Edited by Yukiko Tanaka

With an Introduction and Biographical Essays by the Editor

The Seal Press $

Published by The Seal Press, P.O. Box 13, Seattle, Washington 98111.

Printed in the United States of America
First Edition
10 9 8 7 6 5 4 3 2 1

All stories and prose selections were originally published in Japanese. We gratefully acknowledge the authors and authors' estates for permission to translate and publish these works.

The publication of *To Live and To Write* is made possible in part by a grant from the National Endowment for the Arts.

Library of Congress Cataloging-in-Publication Data

  To live and to write.

  1. Japanese literature—20th century. 2. Japanese literature—Women authors. 3. Women authors, Japanese—Biography. I. Tanaka, Yukiko.
PL726.6.T58   1987   895.6'08'09287   87-4595
ISBN 0-931188-44-X
ISBN 0-931188-43-1 (pbk.)

The cover photograph is of Hayashi Fumiko.
Cover design by Deborah Brown.
Book design by Laurie Becharas and Faith Conlon.

CONTENTS

Acknowledgements

Selecting works to compile an anthology is always a difficult and time-consuming process. I have spent innumerable hours deciding, changing my mind and finally settling on ten narratives to represent one of the most fascinating periods in modern Japanese history. I was fortunate to enlist two excellent translators to participate in this project, but the decision on the selections, and the burden of responsibility, is entirely mine.

Among the people I owe gratitude, I particularly want to thank Ruth Rosenfelder and Arlene Corey, who read the manuscript in its early stages and made many suggestions; Faith Conlon of Seal Press, who has been patient with me during my undertaking of the project, and Katherine Hanson, who supplied helpful editorial comments. I would also like to thank the authors and other individuals who gave me permission to translate and publish the works included in this volume.

Yukiko Tanaka
Seattle, Washington
December 1986

INTRODUCTION

After *This Kind of Woman**, a collection of short stories by contemporary Japanese women writers, was published in 1982, one reader remarked that she had found the stories to be somewhat depressing. The women in the stories, she said, were portrayed as victims of society, passively conforming and enduring their unhappy lot; there was little that suggested the struggle of women to resist and rebel against stifling roles and repressive circumstances. Was this an accurate picture of Japanese women in the 1960s and 70s? the reader asked.

I was taken aback by this question, for indeed one of our objectives in selecting the stories had been to present contemporary Japanese women in a wide range of experiences. That the stories should collectively leave such an impression had never occurred to me. Yet I soon realized that there was a logical explanation for these observations. During the 1960s and early 70s, the period represented in *This Kind of Woman*, few significant intellectual or literary developments took place in Japan. Like the 1950s in the United States, it was a relatively dormant period both socially and culturally, in part because the nation's unprecedented economic development focused attention on material growth.

Reinforcing images of submissive or reticent Japanese women had been far from the intent in compiling the first collection, and I felt it necessary to introduce the Western reader to Japanese women who were strong, independent individuals, determined to shape their own futures. There was a time in the history of modern Japan when women, in search of a

---

* *This Kind of Woman: Ten Stories by Japanese Women Writers*, 1960–1976, edited by Yukiko Tanaka and Elizabeth Hanson (Stanford: Stanford University Press, 1982).

new, more satisfying way to live their lives, raised their voices in opposition to sexual oppression. There were writers among them and they left us a body of literature alive with feminist themes and independent voices. Nine of them—Tamura Toshiko, Miyamoto Yuriko, Hirabayashi Taiko, Hayashi Fumiko, Nakamoto Takako, Nogami Yaeko, Sata Ineko, Uno Chiyo, Okamoto Kanoko*—have been chosen for this new anthology, *To Live and To Write*.

In the years between 1913 and 1938, the period represented in this collection, Japan enjoyed political liberalism after four decades of frantic efforts toward modernization. Individualism and social realism, introduced from the West by the intellectuals of the previous generation, was finding expression in Japanese literature—as was a growing feminist consciousness. The *Seitō-sha*, or Bluestocking Society, organized by Hiratsuka Raichō in 1911 to publish a women's literary magazine, began taking up a number of social and political issues affecting women—from the institution of marriage to abortion to prostitution. In 1922, after a campaign of over three decades, Japanese women finally achieved the revision of the Peace Preservation Act, which allowed them to join political groups and actively participate in politics. They would, however, have to wait until 1945 to obtain the right to vote.

Even when it was illegal to do so, women had always participated in political activities, but during the 1920s and early 1930s increasing numbers of working women joined unions and became a major force in the growing labor movement. In 1927, women in a factory called Tōyō Muslin organized a strike that became an important victory for the labor movement. Women also made gains in education and professional training: In 1925 Japan's first publicly supported medical school for women was opened, and in 1938 the first woman was licensed for to practice law.

Along with these social and political changes, the Japanese lifestyle altered considerably. Running water and gas for

---

*The forms of all names in the volume follow Japanese practice: last (family) name first, then given name.

cooking, as well as public services such as streetcars and tele-
phones, became more readily available, at least in the larger
cities. Western-style recreational and cultural activities were
widely practiced—the café, or coffee house, for instance, became extremely popular. In general, Japanese society was
moving steadily forward in its modernization efforts, and the
country continued in this direction until the Manchurian Incident in 1931, which marked the rise of a more repressive,
xenophobic government. Toward the end of the 1930s, as the
military state prepared for war, women were forced to retreat
to the narrowly defined roles of "good wives and wise mothers"; they were mobilized into patriotic activities and urged to
support the nation's effort by bearing more children.

Literary historians agree that modern Japanese writers did
not regard themselves as social critics until the 1920s. Until
those years, most writers were more interested in artistic development than social change. But the waves of social unrest
after World War I, particularly the succession of strikes and
riots that resulted from widespread economic depression and
high unemployment, made it impossible for Japanese intellectuals to remain silent observers. Leftist ideology swept across
the Japanese intellectual and literary communities until the to-
talitarian government finally suppressed and silenced both
writers and activists in the 1930s.

Hirabayashi Taiko, Miyamoto Yuriko, Sata Ineko and Nakamoto Takako were among those women writers who
joined male activists in the leftist movements. They introduced a woman's point of view into leftist literature by defining themselves as doubly oppressed under the patriarchal system—in the family and in society. These writers, many of
whom came from impoverished families in rural regions,
showed a tenacity and honesty rarely seen among male writers; they observed and wrote about a society run by men and
recorded their personal battles against traditional mores with
unprecedented candor. Hayashi Fumiko, an important writer
of this period but not a part of the leftist school, was catapulted
into prominence by her stories of women's aspirations and
struggles. Though it was short-lived, the leftist literary move-

ment gave Japanese women writers an opportunity to support each other and to speak openly about their lives as women. That they were brought together is particularly significant in view of the crippling isolation in which all Japanese women, writers included, were living prior to this period.

Isolation in a literary world dominated by men and the resulting creative insecurity were major obstacles for Tamura Toshiko, whose work opens this volume. In 1913 she started writing autobiographical stories that described the difficulties faced by a woman artist. The women characters she created represent the first literary endeavor to portray a truly modern woman able to explore her sense of self and her sexuality. Tamura presented in her fiction a dilemma familiar to us today, that of being caught between two worlds, the one socially acceptable but confining, and the other whose new horizons offer both freedom and new difficulties.

Tamura's productive period ended before the end of the 1920s, but she maintained friendships with a number of younger writers who emerged in the 1920s and 30s. Among them were Okamoto Kanoko and Uno Chiyo, whose stories are also included in this book. Less influenced by radical politics than many of their contemporaries, Okamoto and Uno continued to write and publish after the heyday of the leftist movement. Nonetheless, they benefited from the liberal mood of the 1920s and their fiction shows a confidence and strength that is missing in the literature of the 1960s and 1970s. Nogami Yaeko, represented in this book with a short essay, added another dimension to women's fiction, namely a sure sense of the Western literary tradition of nineteenth century realism. Unaffected by either political ideology or current literary trends, Okamoto, Uno and Nogami follow a line of women writers, liberated in their view of female sexuality, dating back to the pre-fuedal era of the twelfth century.

With the exception of Tamura, all of the women represented in this volume wrote actively during the post World War II era. Uno, Sata and Nakamoto, all in their eighties and nineties, are still writing today.

Itō Sei, a critic, novelist and the author of a major study of modern Japanese literature, has pointed out that the main stream of modern Japanese writing is tied up with the personal experience of the writer—and that this must be appreciated if one is to understand the special nature of Japanese prose-writing. The autobiographical form has indeed been the most basic and persisting approach to Japanese fiction writing since the turn of the century. Living and writing—these two activities have been much more difficult to separate for modern Japanese authors than for their counterparts in the West. A great deal of Japanese fiction written in the first half of the twentieth century is based on personal experience, as is the case with the prose collected in this volume. Often undramatic and sometimes loosely plotted, such works may at first seem peculiar to Western literary tastes, but read within a certain frame of reference, they help reveal the depth and define the contours of modern Japanese life and literature.

Most of the pieces chosen for this book belong to the earliest periods of their author's careers; most were originally published in literary magazines current at the time. Although sometimes executed with less skill than works written later, the selections reveal important aspects of the authors' lives and focus on themes of women's creativity and autonomy. As a collection, they also reflect the period in which they were written, a time when Japanese society experienced social and political liberalism for the first time in its modern history. Biographical essays on the authors have been included to place the writings in their historical context and to supply the reader with background information. Together with the selections themselves, they provide an introduction to the accomplishments of nine outstanding women writers who fought to achieve personal freedom and artistic independence—to live and to write.

Yukiko Tanaka

TO LIVE AND TO WRITE

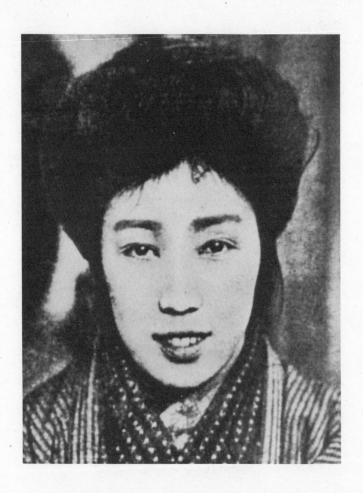

Tamura Toshiko

(1884-1945)

1911 WAS A MEMORABLE YEAR in the history of Japanese women's emancipation, particularly for those involved in writing. In September of that year, a twenty-five-year-old woman started a feminist magazine with the help of her friends and one hundred yen, which her mother had given her from her own savings. The woman was Hiratsuka Haru, later known as Hiratsuka Raichō, and her magazine, *Bluestocking* (*Seitō*), created a stir among many women of her generation. In 1916, pressure from society's conservative forces, chief among them educational institutions and government bureaucrats, forced the magazine to shut down. But by that time *Seitō* had become a symbol of Japan's "New Woman." Although *Seitō* did not contribute as much to discovering and promoting the creative talents of women as it originally avowed, it did provide a forum where women affirmed their solidarity and expressed their revolt against old social and family mores.

One year before the first publication of *Seitō*, a woman named Tamura Toshiko established herself as a writer with the publication of her story, "Resignation" (*Akirame*), which won a competition prize in the national newspaper *Asahi*. Within a few years she was considered among the most talented of women writers, one who was able to achieve critical recognition in the literary world. Though not actively involved with Raichō's feminist group, Toshiko wrote stories with similar themes of protest against male domination over women, and her work appeared in the first issue of *Bluestocking*. Drawn to writing fiction out of a need for self-discovery and self-expression, she tried to depict the conflict between the old and the new as she herself felt them. "Vow" (*Seigon*, 1912), for instance, is about a woman who leaves her husband because he,

5

like other men, oppresses her, albeit unconsciously. In her attempt to gain independence, the woman in this story declares defiantly: "My attitude is mine, and my personality, whether or not people are disgusted or repulsed by it, is also mine."

The majority of Toshiko's works are autobiographical and her heroines are often characterized by Toshiko's own deep-seated ambivalence. In the very early stage of writing Toshiko embodied various facets of her personality in different characters. In "Resignation," for instance, she divided herself into three sisters, Tsumako, Tomie and Kie. The narrative is told from the point of view of Tomie, who decides to return to her home town to fulfill her filial duty despite her potentially promising future as a screenwriter. Her sister Tsumako is a subservient wife whose husband tries to flirt with the other sister, Kie. Though the basic mood of the story is that of surrender, "Resignation" also describes the subtlety of a young woman's awakening to her sense of self. It is interesting to note that Tomie's self-awareness is, in part, achieved through her relationship with her girlfriend, and the story is the first in modern Japanese fiction to explore the sensuous nature of a young woman's attraction to another woman.

Many of Toshiko's better works were produced through her internal struggles over the dichotomy of independence and dependence, and through the more real difficulties she experienced in her marital conflicts. The desire to break away and establish an independent identity is countered by a longing for the protection and comfort dependency offers, a theme illustrated by Toshiko's fine story, "Painted Lips of Mummies" (*Miirā no Kuchibeni*, 1913). Toshiko's works often portray a dead-end relationship between a man and a woman, and examine the woman's self-destructive approach in dealing with her frustration, anger and fear. For example, in "A Woman Writer" (*Onna Sakusha*, 1913), the protagonist attempts to analyze the origins of her feelings of disgust toward herself and her lover, and realizes how tenuous her self-identity really is. Although Toshiko tried to present these conflicts symbolically, writing was often painfully difficult for her.

Some women writers, including Raichō, were critical of Toshiko's work because her heroines were indecisive and ambivalent, and because the stories were without a constructive message. These critics did acknowledge Toshiko's technical mastery, but even so, their criticism was not well founded. Although Toshiko's stories may lack single-minded, resolute characters and clear themes, they do ring true to life as she saw it. Drawing from her own experiences, Toshiko succeeded in creating a more complex portrait of a woman's search for self and her struggle for independence than any other Japanese woman writer before her.

Like many other Japanese women writers, Toshiko's interest in writing began early, and by the time she was thirteen or so she was writing sentimental stories. She was also an avid reader, though her reading list did not include Western literature; instead she tended to read popular fiction. Her childhood and adolescent years were spent in a section of Tokyo where old, plebeian culture remained entrenched and this very likely affected Toshiko's later lifestyle. Not much is known about her father except that he deserted his wife and two small children. Her younger sister died at an early age and afterwards Toshiko lived alone with her mother. Not a top but a good student in high school, Toshiko entered the newly established Japan Women's College only to withdraw within a year, perhaps because financial support from her father was discontinued. She rarely spoke of her father or mother, even to close friends. However, the character of her mother, the daughter of a rice merchant, appears quite frequently in Toshiko's stories as a selfish and vain woman who indulges in her own pleasure rather than thinking of her child's welfare.

At eighteen Toshiko became a protégé of Kōda Rohan, a writer known for his elegant, traditional style and his penchant for old-fashioned stoicism. He gave Toshiko little guidance except to strongly discourage her against reading contemporary fiction. In the tradition of her mentor, Toshiko wrote a number of stories in a pseudo-classical style. These were published, but Toshiko had decided that writing was not the best way to achieve social recognition and so she temporarily abandoned it in favor of something more promising and glamorous. She took up acting and worked in a variety of small companies, including one called the New Society Theater. There were few educated woman who became actresses in those days, partly because the traditional kabuki theater was restricted to male actors and partly because stage performance in general was considered a vulgar form of entertainment. In a Western-influenced play called *The Wave* (*Nami*), Toshiko played the leading role, a successful concert pianist who is torn between her love and her career. The play was well received but the production was not financially successful, and the company was soon disbanded. Toshiko found the world of actors and actresses disappointingly unstimulating, and lost interest.

While a student of Rohan, Toshiko had developed an interest in another aspiring writer, Tamura Shōgyo. Shōgyo had spent a number of years in the United States, and when he returned in 1909, he and Toshiko were married. This did not turn out to be a harmonious marriage, however. Shōgyo was not a successful writer and Toshiko resented the fact that she had to shoulder the responsibility of supporting them both, since she was by this time enjoying considerable success as a short story writer. A number of Toshiko's better works are, in fact, based on her relentless evaluation of her troubled relationship with Shōgyo.

Toshiko finally left Shōgyo in 1916. By this time the problematic marriage had ceased to provide Toshiko with creative inspiration. She continued to produce new works, still using her fiction as a mirror of her own self-scrutiny, but it was all too clear, not least to herself, that her career was in sharp decline. Financially, she found herself in a precarious situation for, though writing did bring her a good income, she squandered it on luxury items and was forever in debt. "Glory" (*Eiga*), a story she wrote the same year she left Shōgyo, tells the story of a proud woman whose potential good life and independence were wasted in self-destructive indulgence. In "The Snake" (*Hebi*), another story Toshiko wrote that year, the actress heroine finds that her fading career has reduced her to perform on stage half-naked, with a snake wrapped around her; she yearns for the appearance of the ideal man to rescue her from her miserable life.

Unable to write and barely supporting herself by making dolls—a skill she had learned as a girl—Toshiko met in 1917 Suzuki Etsu, a writer and journalist who was two years her junior and married. A passionate love affair ensued and a year later Toshiko did not hesitate to follow Etsu to Vancouver, British Columbia, where he had found a job as a journalist with a Japanese newspaper. Inasmuch as adultery was a punishable crime in Japan at the time, this was a reasonable course for the two lovers to take. They stayed in Canada for the next eighteen years.

When Toshiko arrived in Vancouver, there were two thousand Japanese immigrants in the city and their newspaper, *The Continental Daily News*, had about thirty employees. The years in Vancouver with Etsu were happy ones for Toshiko. Her husband was an honored and respected member of the Japanese community and she assumed her role as wife and hostess wholeheartedly. She became a leader among the women in the community, helping them to organize various volunteer activities, which ranged from arts events to classes on birth control methods. Although Toshiko wrote almost no fiction during these Vancouver years (one single piece was published in *The Continental Daily News*), her pen was not inactive. She contributed poems and short essays to the newspaper under the name *tori no ko* (a little bird), and when Etsu started his own newspaper, called *The People*, Toshiko became his able assistant, taking over when he fell ill. She also wrote during this period a number of *waka* poems, traditional verse with thirty-one syllables.

In 1932, tragedy struck. Etsu, who had returned to Japan, suddenly died. Toshiko was devastated. She left Vancouver and tried to re-establish herself in Los Angeles, but this met with failure. In 1936 she returned to Japan, where she once again turned to writing fiction. Her stories about Japanese immigrants and her experiences in California, unfortunately, did not find an audience among the readers who had enjoyed her stories several decades earlier. Still, her admirers had not forgotten her and among these were a number of prominent women writers, including Okamoto Kanoko, Sata Ineko, and Enchi Fumiko.

At the end of 1938, deeply in debt and once again amorously involved with a married man, Toshiko traveled alone to China on the invitation of the Japanese military. After visiting several major cities, she settled in Shanghai, where she took a job as the editor of *Women's Voice* (*Josei*), a magazine for Chinese women that was sponsored by the Japanese occupational government. Publishing became difficult, however, almost as soon as she started, and her health deteriorated. She was alone in a taxi when a heart attack struck her. She died two days later in the hospital.

Perhaps more successfully than any other woman writer of the twentieth century's early decades, Toshiko delineated the dilemma of Japanese women who yearned both for the independence and freedom of the "New Women" on the one hand, and the security of the old traditions on the other. Her stories of a woman's social, intellectual and sexual awakening made her one of the most admired writers of her times. Two decades after her death, the Tamura Toshiko Literary Prize was established by her friends, with the royalty money her stories continued to earn.

Y. T.

A Woman Writer

translated by Yukiko Tanaka

The head of this woman writer was filled with refuse. She had squeezed all the wits out of her brain, and no matter how hard she wrung it, her bag of wits offered not so much as a single word that was alive nor half a phrase that smelled of warm blood. She had been trying to write a story commissioned by a magazine ever since the end of last year; she pushed an idea around but found it unmanageable. All day long she sat behind her desk, yet produced nothing but a pattern of flax leaves and vertical lines to fit the squares where letters ought to be written.

The room where the woman writer sat, a charcoal brazier by her side, was a four-and-a-half-mat room on the second floor. One day a strong wind blew hour after hour, enough to tear everything apart, but another day a weak sun shone sleepily through the rice-paper screen, an obscure, lusterless sun that looked as if it would disappear with one swipe. On such a day the sky was opaque with barely a hint of color, shining only on the surface. Still the sky was quiet and soft, and seemed to smile at the trees in the forest which, having surrendered to the authority of winter, exposed themselves, naked and unsightly. The sky turned its gentle smile toward the woman writer, who kept gazing outside; she was somehow reminded of the face of her lover. The sky was like the gentle and generous smile that spread over his face, the smile that never showed a trace of ridicule in his large intelligent eyes.

The woman writer felt as if she were being pulled by the sleeve, a force unexpectedly calling her attention to something dear to her heart. She breathed all her emotion into her smiling mouth, keeping her eyes wide open, and a spontaneous sensation of affection toward her lover came to her like the gentle stimulus of a face brush on her skin. It was like a glimpse of the soft flow of celadon green peeking out from under the sleeve of a white silk garment; it sent out a wonderful feeling, simple, old-fashioned and graceful. And the woman writer, who wanted to toy with this sensation and satisfy her fickle mood, closed her eyes in order to capture the image of the man and carry it into the depths of her mind's eye. She wanted to hold the image tightly after she fondled it in the palm of her hand. And then she threw the image into the sky to gaze at it from a distance. Filling the paper with letters became, as a consequence, a job even more irksome.

The woman writer used powder all the time. Even though she was about to reach thirty, she wore heavy makeup. When no one was around, she made up her face like a stage actress and secretly enjoyed looking at herself in the mirror. She could not do without face powder, and in fact even wore it when she was in bed, as long as she didn't feel too ill. When she had no powder on her face, she felt as if she were dragging around something ugly and bare on her body. When she didn't wear face powder, her emotions became jagged; she felt awful, unduly suspicious, and it showed in her expressions. Her mood deteriorated; she became sulky and lost all desire to be flirtatious. She feared this state more than anything else. And that was why she had to cover her naked face with powder all the time. She enjoyed the faint scent when the powder, mixed with a little bit of her own body oils, stirred in the air around her nose or cheek. The pleasing smell of the powder opened her eyes to things around her; her mind became saturated by its aura and, coquetry emanating from her body, she adored herself.

The woman writer did not forget to make up her face even on days when she had a great deal of difficulty with the writing she had promised to do. She knew that as she prepared the powder in front of the mirror, ideas often came to her. When she touched the tip of her finger to the powder melted in the water, the cold sensation seemed to release a refreshing image in her mind, and as she went on brushing the powder on her face, the idea slowly developed. This had happened more than times. Most of her writing, therefore, had been born out of face powder, and so it had the smell of powder.

Recently, however, no idea had come to her, even with face powder. Just as her skin underneath the powder felt dry and cracked, she no longer felt that particular yearning, that sensation of warm blood swirling up within her flesh. Her bloodshot eyes sunk in and her cheeks swelled, giving her the look of a badger made of spun sugar. She couldn't put her finger on what was wrong. There was nothing to write about; it was impossible to write anything: that was all she could think of. Then she began to feel desperate; she had a creepy sensation of soft hands with long, spidery fingernails wrapping around her neck, choking her.

So finally, this morning, the woman writer broke down and cried in front of her husband.

"I've never felt so miserable. I'm going to run away somewhere. Tell them whatever you think will satisfy them. I can't write one more page."

"It doesn't concern me," the husband finally said. He had been smoking by the charcoal brazier. His feigned indifference revealed his small-mindedness—a shabby revenge. He was clearly thinking that it was she who used to boast of her independence: *At one time you said that you'd pursue your own course and not ask for my help.* Looking at him deliberately sticking out his small chin, the woman writer felt as if the flesh on her face were being stripped away, exposing the bare bones.

"What did you say?" she said, nonetheless, with a decisive voice that shot straight out through her misery. She stared him squarely in the face.

"I said it's none of my business. Think about it. What have you written this year? How many hundreds of pages did you write last year, hmm? You can't say there's nothing to write about. I have no hope for you. If I were to write, forty or fifty pages a day would be easy; there are a million things to write about, all around you. You can write about anything—the neighbors' sons and their sibling rivalry, the younger brother kicking his older brother out of the house, something like that. It's easy. Women are no good, wasting a hundred pages in order to write ten or twenty pages, and spending ten or fifteen days only for that. You must think you're a great writer." The woman's husband kept this up, his voice assailing her like cheap clogs clattering over the stepping stones. As she listened, the woman writer's eyes widened and her eyebrows lifted higher. She no longer felt like crying and started laughing instead.

"I understand. But I'm really surprised to hear that from a person who also used to be a writer," she said.

The woman writer hopped around the room, kicking the bottom of her kimono, her arms still tucked in the sleeves. The tears at the edges of her eyes were cold. As she hopped about passing back and forth in front of the full-length mirror, she caught a glimpse of herself, looking like a flying shuttlecock. She continued for a while, enjoying the colors at the tip of the skirt dancing around her feet, but the fun was soon taken over by an impulse to be petulant, to torment someone; she felt a part of her body contracting, she felt provoked. She turned to her husband and thrust her face at him, baring her teeth. Then, putting her knuckles against his forehead, she pushed him. He pretended to take no notice.

"Look here—a clown, a jester, and the demon's face."

The husband still didn't say a word. The woman writer put her knee against his back and pushed, and as he had been squatting in front of the charcoal brazier, he fell onto the floor. He got up right away, however, and resumed the same posture as before, extending his hands over the fire.

"Hey, you, hey," she said in a low voice, and grabbed his collar to pull him backward. "Take this off, undress," she said, pulling his kimono as hard as she could. When the husband pushed her hand away, she thrust her hand into his mouth and tore at his lips. As she felt the wet warmth of the inside of his

mouth at the tip of her fingers, a flash ran through her: the
memory of the moment when her body and mind were loosened under this man's fingers. The next moment, she pulled
her hand out of his mouth and pinched his cheek as if she were
trying to wrench it out of his face. The husband, who was used
to the explosive behavior of his wife, remained silent. He
looked as though he was thinking, *What a vixen she is*, but the
stubborn expression on his closed lips revealed that he knew
he should leave her alone.

After she pushed her husband's head once more, the woman
writer went upstairs to her room. The fire in the charcoal brazier was the color of melted ruby. The coals were as red as ripe
pomegranates and the rising air shimmered above them. She
went to her desk, a beautiful object of lacquered papier-mâ-
ché, decorated with plum flowers made from pearl-oyster
shells. As she sat there, she felt her entire body go limp, as if all
of her blood were draining out of it. She felt terribly sad and
started to cry.

"What a bad woman," she heard herself saying over and
over while she cried.

The woman writer was thinking that she was the most
worthless among all of her girlfriends. Then she remembered
a friend who had come to see her a few days ago, looking very
smug. Her friend had told her that she was going to marry and
that she and her future husband would live separately. They
were deeply in love, but they had decided not to live together;
they had agreed to live apart and to be in love for the rest of
their lives.

"Even though I am getting married, I will remain myself, I
am I. The love I have is not for the sake of anyone else. It's for
myself. It's my love," this friend said to the woman writer.
When she talked, her crooked teeth showed slightly. Overwhelmed by her friend's words, the woman writer couldn't
say anything for a while.

"You often complain of the pain, but you've somehow resolved it within yourself, haven't you? That's fine, then. Even
if it's painful, you've settled with yourself. I can't give in and
disregard my ego. I am I. So, I've decided that when I want to

see him, I'll see him. When I don't, I won't," the friend continued.

"But you will think of the man you're going to marry every single day; you cannot do otherwise," said the woman writer. Her friend simply said "Yes," and peeled an orange, keeping her little fingers straight.

"I feel I have very little sense of myself. If someone pulls me to the right, I'll go to the right. Or to the left. Whatever. I am lazy."

"That's not true. You say that because something just happened and you're reacting to it," said the friend. She put a segment of orange into her mouth.

"I am going to live for myself," she continued. "Self is the art one creates, you see. To live for the sake of one's art is, after all, to live for oneself."

"I feel so awful now that I think of killing myself," said the woman writer. "I don't know what I should live for. I have this feeling that I desperately need something I can hold on to but I don't know what that could be—or how. I've thought of religion; I've thought of becoming a nun rather than living the way I do."

"I've thought about that too. And I came to the conclusion that there's no other way; I must live for myself. And I am going to." The friend left, repeating these words. She wore a long black cloak which belonged to her lover.

The woman writer had in fact considered living alone more than once; she'd been tormented by the idea. But she knew she couldn't do this. It wasn't possible to go back to the life of living alone.

"Why did you get married then?" the friend asked her once.

"He was my first love," the woman writer answered.

"Well, then you had no choice," the friend said. The woman writer had wanted to say something more to her girlfriend, but didn't. She simply smiled.

First love—it had happened when she was nineteen. It might not have been real love but merely that her flirtatious nature made her go after a man. Nonetheless, there was no mistaking that a tiny bud in her heart, accidentally torn open by this young lover years ago, was still there; it sat in a corner of her heart, quietly casting its shadow. Whatever warmth remained in her heart toward the man she lived with came from a drop of dew shed by the broken bud. She knew that the dew would continue to drop as long as she lived. Even if she left him and lived alone, the moisture that penetrated her heart would remind her of her lover and lead her back to him.

The woman writer did not tell this to her girlfriend. The naiveté of her friend, who seemed to be trying a marriage that would exclude a carnal relationship, affected her. She didn't know what kind of man the friend's lover was. According to what someone had told her, he was an artist who belonged to the school of New Art. What sort of things would her friend say one year from now? the woman writer wondered. She realized she felt somehow threatened by her friend's proclamation of strength and her belief in the idea of living one's own life.

Coming back to herself, the woman writer looked at the white paper in front of her. She must write something, but what. . . ?

"You are no good"—the exact words her husband had uttered earlier—came back to her. Why did she laugh? she wondered. His remark was silly, but why had she not said something back to him then? She felt rebellious.

"What do you mean 'I'm no good,'" she wanted to tell him now in order to pick another quarrel. She wanted to get herself into a state—it didn't matter how—so that her emotions could violently churn; she wanted to rip herself open. She should make her husband even more angry, she said to herself.

He's like a whetstone, the woman writer thought. No matter how fragrant a vapor she sent off, he absorbed it in an instant, and then, only a dry, uninteresting surface remained.

"I'll leave you," she could say, and he would no doubt answer, "All right."

If she were to say that she loved him after all, he would simply respond, "I see." He was like that. Whatever he saw passing in front of his eyes, whatever crossed his mind, he would let it go, let it slide by; he didn't care. His body must be filled with sawdust. The circulation of his blood, where the essence of life streamed, must be obstructed. If so, the woman thought now, there was no sense in going downstairs to confront him.

The next day, the woman writer sat at the desk again. It was raining but she heard no sound of rain except intermittent large drops hitting the windowpane. Occasionally the wind blew against the paper screen, making it flap. She was reminded of a friend who had promised to visit her on a rainy day. This thought passed without stirring up anything more interesting in her mind. She then remembered an actress of whom she was very fond. The actress had been making cold radish salad on the stage. Her hands had looked so cold and red. *I wanted to hold her hands in mine and warm them with my lips. . . .*

Original title: *Onna Sakusha* (1913).

Glory

translated by Yukiko Tanaka

- I -

Having lost almost everything she had, Komatsu couldn't think of a single thing she might be able to exchange for cash. She decided to go to Nonose to ask for a loan, and waited till evening to take a rickshaw to Yūrakucho.

"It's quite late. Are you on your way back from somewhere?" Kaneko, Nonose's wife, said in an ingratiating voice as she greeted her with a smile. There wasn't a touch of unfriendliness in her spirited, dark-complexioned face. Nonose himself was in bed with a cold.

"Where have you been? You didn't come from your house, I know. Not at this hour," Kaneko went on. Her smiling eyes implied that she knew where Komatsu had been. Avoiding the question, Komatsu kept her eyes absent-mindedly on Kaneko's hand pouring tea into a cup. There was something reliable and calming in Kaneko's manner that made her feel like confiding in her and telling her about what was happening in her life. Kaneko was now talking about the Cock Fair she'd been to but, suddenly remembering something, she went to the chest of drawers in the next room and came back with some fabric wrapped in a large scarf.

"This is the fabric you gave me. It's been dyed a very pretty color. Take a look. I know my dark complexion, so I had it dyed like this. Do you think it looks good on me?" Kaneko asked, spreading the fabric in front of Komatsu. Some time

19

ago Komatsu had given her some cloth of plain silk crepe, and Kaneko had had it dyed. Komatsu took the cloth in her hand and said it was a nice color. Kaneko then brought a kimono out of the drawer, a kimono Komatsu had given her. She said she had to re-stitch it.

"You have a lot of kimonos, certainly you don't need to go to all that trouble," Komatsu said, forcing a smile, as she looked at the kimono in Kaneko's hand.

A lamp was hanging right above Komatsu's head and the light shining on her face bothered her; the headache she had felt since she entered Kaneko's house was getting worse. When Kaneko went to the dimly lit adjacent room to put the kimono away, Komatsu followed her there and brought up the subject of the loan.

"All right, I'll go and ask my husband," Kaneko said, and went upstairs. Komatsu returned to the charcoal brazier and sat down; she was gazing at the brand-new, red bamboo rake placed on the top of the china cabinet when Nonose came in. He greeted Komatsu in a polite manner, and then sat where his wife had been, looking uncomfortable in his quilted gown. His handsome face, with its prominent nose and a firm mouth, looked a bit blurred, perhaps because of the heaviness around his feverish eyes. When he tried to breathe through his nose, he lifted his face slightly toward the light.

"You've got a cold."

"Yes," he said, and was silent for a while, smoking a pipe.

"Old Mrs. Toda was here the day before yesterday," he then said as he knocked the ashes from the pipe on the corner of the brazier.

"What did she want?"

"She wanted to talk about Mieko. She wants custody."

Komatsu turned her pretty eyes up to Nonose and waited.

"She heard that you're still behaving badly; she thinks it's harmful for Mieko—for her future—to live with you."

Komatsu looked down, offended. Kaneko came into the room quietly and put some charcoal into the brazier.

"If I say 'no,' she can't have her," said Komatsu after a while, forcing herself to speak. She felt angry and reckless.

"But you must give it serious thought. How do you think you can manage, if you have Mieko to provide for? You've lost everything. What if it gets to the point of not having enough to get by? Even if you could scrape along, it's not fair to Mieko, don't you agree?"

"I know that," she said, flustered. It was painful to listen to Nonose point out her situation to her. She was feeling desperate, as if a fire had been set on her back.

At Komatsu's interruption, Nonose frowned and sipped the tea his wife had served. Then he looked intently at the expensive silk crepe kimono Komatsu wore and at the pale, hollow cheeks that revealed the anguish she suffered from her love affair. A few loose strands of soft hair caressed her cheek.

"I'd made up my mind not to meddle in your affairs, and so I told Mrs. Toda that she should talk to you directly. But since you're here I thought I should let you know."

Komatsu did not respond.

Nonose had worked for Komatsu's late husband as his business manager, and so he was in and out of the Toda house a great deal. People had talked about Nonose, insinuating that he, a good-looking man, was having an affair with Komatsu. After his employer's death, Nonose had tried to support and advise Komatsu, who had found herself in a difficult position living with her cynical mother-in-law and arrogant brother-in-law and his wife. Komatsu chose to go her own way, indulging herself at the theaters and teahouses she used to frequent with her husband, a man notorious for his reckless extravagance. There she was as lavish with her money as he had been. People thought that Nonose and his wife fawned over Komatsu, encouraging her to throw her money away. When this rumor reached Nonose, he stopped going to the Todas.

Five years after her husband's death, Komatsu left the Toda house, taking her younger child, Mieko, with her and leaving her son, Junichi, behind. Even then, Nonose had kept himself out of Komatsu's life. He had heard that Komatsu was having an affair with a kabuki actor. He also knew that she had quickly exhausted the remaining assets given to her at the time of her leaving the Todas, and that she had been selling her personal belongings with the help of his wife. But he hadn't said a word to Komatsu, maintaining his position of simply observing.

For some reason Nonose now found himself thinking of the past, of everything that had happened between himself and the Todas. He sincerely wanted to help Komatsu for the sake of bygone times, to demonstrate his unfailing sense of duty. Looking at her sitting in front of him, sunk in her fortunes, he couldn't help feeling despondent himself: it was her imprudence, he reflected, that had made her ignore his concern. As she sat there forlornly, her head bowed, Nonose could see the naiveté of an unworldly person and the shyness of a young girl; he was touched by it. He looked away for a while, not knowing what to say.

"Why don't you talk about Mieko some other time? Komatsu needs money, and rather urgently, I'm sure," Kaneko said, hesitating. Nonose, still silent, clapped his head a few times with his hand and rubbed his forehead.

"We don't have any extra money but still we should be able to . . ." Kaneko went on. There was both kindness and chatty sociability in her eagerness. After a while Nonose told Kaneko to fetch his satchel; he took ten five-yen bills out of it and handed them over to Komatsu.

"In the days when I worked for Mr. Toda, people thought I made a great deal of money. But for some reason I'm still poor. After giving you these ten bills, nothing's left," he said with a wry smile. Then he excused himself, saying he had a bad chill.

Komatsu felt relieved to be left alone with Kaneko, and looked at her fondly.

"You shouldn't worry too much. Things will work out one way or another. You're used to luxury, so there's no use telling you to be frugal with money, I'm sure," Kaneko said, and started cooking some rice cakes she had bought at the Cock Fair on the brazier. While they were cooking, she asked about Mieko and Otoku, the old woman who worked for Komatsu.

"You're still young, and quite pretty. Your future's in your hands. A flower yet to bloom, you know. You don't need to worry."

Kaneko's words sounded so hopeful that the pain and depression Komatsu had felt earlier sitting in front of Nonose went away, and a gorgeous scene from her past unfurled before her eyes. It was not possible that adversity could invade such a brilliant world. She stared at the empty space in front of her; her eyes darkened with rebellion. It was as if she were trying not to see the dreadful pit that was her fate and into which she was slowly falling.

"You still wear that pin," said Kaneko, referring to the ornament Komatsu wore in her hair. Komatsu put her hand to her head and touched a gold hairpin with a diamond inset. She pulled the pin out, a faint smile on her face, and put it on her lap.

"You can go on selling your things for a while at least."

"No, there's nothing left anymore. Everything's gone. I somehow overlooked this one."

Indeed, there had been no rings on her fingers for some time now.

"You're not that badly off, even so. If you sell this pin, you can easily get as much as my husband just gave you.

"I don't need it anyway. I'll leave it with you. I know your husband needs the money he's given me, so if you can do something with it, please go ahead," said Komatsu, handing the pin to Kaneko.

"You only think there's nothing left. More pins like this will appear from drawers, I'm sure," said Kaneko, smiling.

– 2 –

Otoku was still up sewing when Komatsu returned home. A dark gloominess seemed to permeate the house, and this made Komatsu angry; her light-hearted mood suddenly dissipated. She sat facing Otoku, who didn't say a word, but kept on sewing. Komatsu watched her for a while as if in trance, still lost in her dreams. The old woman looked stern and cross as usual.

Otoku was fifty and had a great deal of grey hair for her age. She piled her hair high and arranged it over a comb; her face was smooth, pale and slightly swollen. She was sewing a red undergarment for Mieko, her two hands barely showing out from under her sleeves. As she watched the large body of Otoku as she continued to sew with her head down, Komatsu felt sorry for her. Her sullen face looked particularly dejected that night. Both sat there, silent, for a long time till Komatsu finally said that they should go to bed, and started to undress.

When Otoku insisted that she wanted to sew more, Komatsu went back to the charcoal brazier and sat down, throwing her kimono around her shoulders.

"Old Mrs. Toda wants custody of Mieko. I just heard about it at the Nonoses tonight," Komatsu said. She knew that Otoku didn't respond readily these days when Komatsu spoke to her, although she would open her mouth when necessary. And yet she wanted to talk with Otoku, who loved Mieko as if she were her own child; she wanted to share her anxiety over the custody question. She said emphatically, as she had at the Nonoses, that under no circumstances would she give Mieko up.

"What could they be thinking? Asking for Mieko on top of Junichi! What a selfish mother-in-law I have, really. I won't let her go, you know," said Komatsu, hoping for some supportive words from Otoku. But there was no response.

"I think she'd be happier there," said Otoku after a while.

"Living with the Todas, you mean?"

"Yes, that's what I mean. If she stays with you, what'll happen to her no one knows. She's be better off living with her grandmother now."

"I see," said Komatsu. There was a faint smile on her face. She looked as if she wanted to say something, but she kept silent. She bowed her head and soon there were tears welling up in her eyes. Otoku didn't seem to notice, even when the tears began running down Komatsu's pretty cheeks.

"You've indulged yourself and gotten into trouble—that's your choice. But Mieko, I pity her. I can see what she'd have to go through if she stayed with you," said Otoku.

"I'm merely a servant, and so if you fire me tomorrow, I can't complain. That's fine. But Mieko is different." Otoku's voice was rough and sharp, spiteful and stubborn.

Otoku had come along as Mieko's nurse when Komatsu left the Todas. She had disliked both the younger brother of Komatsu's late husband and his wife, and had considered it her good fortune that she could live with Mieko and Komatsu. Knowing that Komatsu had received enough to live quite comfortably for the rest of her life, she had hoped to serve her for a long time, at least until Mieko got married, perhaps until Komatsu had grandchildren. She had even looked forward to the day when, in a dozen or so years, she would be able to take care of them. The happiness she dreamed of, however, vanished rather quickly as a result of Komatsu's extravagance. She started to hate her mistress. A woman who had spent, in a year or two, all that money—a sum she herself could never have hoped to earn even if she had worked her entire lifetime and then some more. Such a woman would surely offend the Divine Grace: her mistress would not escape the punishment of Heaven. She was certain that Komatsu, who rarely showed motherly affection for her small child, who instead was infatuated with an actor and had spent her fortune on him, would soon find herself in a wretched life. Ever since she realized that Komatsu, with Kaneko's help, had been selling her personal belongings, she locked the drawers in which Mieko's clothes were kept. She stayed on for Mieko's sake, living day by day, feeling uncertain about her future.

"What do you mean, you pity her? Why do you say that? I haven't yet let you and Mieko go hungry, have I? Do you think I make Mieko suffer? If you think I'm such an unreliable mistress, why, you don't have to stay. You can certainly leave," said Komatsu, flushing. She was trembling with anger from Otoku's words. The warped suspicions and stubborness of this ignorant old woman who knew nothing beyond her lower-class upbringing infuriated Komatsu. "I won't let myself ask favors of you. You don't know anything so why don't you keep your mouth shut?" she said, with her face turned away from Otoku. She was trying to control her anger and as a result she sounded unnaturally forceful.

"If you want me to leave, I'll go any time. I've been staying only for Mieko's sake," answered Otoku. Looking up from her work, she put her sewing away. Her face, with its small round nose and afflicted eyes, reminded Komatsu of a cheap wooden Noh mask. Placing her sewing box on top of a folded red cloth, Otoku stood up and went to her three-mat room next to the kitchen.

Left alone, Komatsu sat gloomily for a while. Her anger toward Otoku evaporated. The old woman's blind love for Mieko and her generally jaundiced view led her to believe that Komatsu had no tender feelings for the child, she reasoned. Otoku seemed to think that some moral lapse in Komatsu was leading to imminent hardship for the three of them. She no longer cared what Otoku thought. There was something else she had to think about, but she couldn't remember what it was. Her head felt heavy and tight. She remembered that she had vaguely considered asking her older brother in Osaka if she and Mieko could live with his family. But it's not that, she said to herself reprovingly, it's something really important.

A life swept away by a huge tidal wave—Komatsu thought she had a glimpse of the awful destination awaiting her. A proud woman once basking in glory was engulfed by a wave, leaving a pathetic-looking woman with a child, a woman who was lost and who didn't know how to get food for the next day. "That can never happen," she murmured. Only yesterday she was at the height of her powers, an attractive woman surrounded by many admirers. She tried to hold on to that fleeting image in order to forget her weak reality. She tried to conjure up the image of Koisaburō, a popular kabuki actor who had always been attentive in her days of prosperity. He was still her lover; she could see him anytime she wanted to. Thinking of this man, the only one who had not betrayed her, gave Komatsu a sense of confidence, as if her glory were still with her. She felt excited.

*   *   *

– 3 –

Komatsu's fretful mood made it difficult for her to stay home, even for a day or two. Getting up in the afternoon in her upstairs room, she thought of the night that was soon to come; she felt dreary, not knowing how to deal with her wretchedness. A gusty, wintery wind blew against the windowpane that filtered the sun, and occasionally falling maple leaves would hit the window, making rustling noises. The money she had gotten from Nonose several days earlier was almost gone. She decided to return to his house, remembering the diamond pin that she had left.

A few days earlier Komatsu had gone to the Chimaki teahouse to see Koisaburō. He hadn't shown up. He had ignored her invitation.

"So ungrateful of him, I must say. But please do come back because tomorrow I will do whatever I can to make him come," the mistress of Chimaki told her. The next day Komatsu had felt so disheartened that she didn't return. But now she felt an urge to go downtown, to see brightly lit streets. The memory of pleasure made Komatsu restless. She was unable to resist the idea of going to Chimaki. She wanted the intoxicating sensation of waiting there for her lover. She got out of bed and went downstairs.

Mieko was sitting alone, eating cookies. Seeing her mother, she came and looked up at Komatsu's face fondly. Komatsu glanced at her daughter, noticing that she was wearing a red ribbon, and went straight to the bathroom to wash her face.

"Where did Otoku go, Mie-chan?" Komatsu asked when she returned from the bathroom. Mieko's answer was so vague that she couldn't guess where the old woman might have gone. She went upstairs again and got ready to go out, thinking that Otoku would return shortly. But Otoku had not come back by the time when Komatsu was ready to leave.

"Where did she say she was going, Mie-chan?" she asked again. Her daughter was still eating cookies by the hallway window.

"I don't know," said Mieko, her mouth full of food.

"Where could she have gone?" Komatsu sat down next to her daughter, uneasy. She began to suspect that Otoku had not gone on an errand.

"About what time did she leave?"

"A little while ago."

"About what time was that?"

"It was a little while ago." Mieko was pleased that her mother put her arms around her.

Komatsu went to Otoku's room. All of her belongings were gone from the closet. "She's left us," Komatsu murmured to herself. Mieko came and stood next to her and looked into the closet like her mother.

"Otoku went back to her home without telling me."

"She went back to her home?"

"Yes, she did. Bad Otoku, don't you think?"

Otoku has left because of what I said to her a few nights ago, Komatsu thought. Annoyed, she looked inside the empty closet again before closing the door. When she returned to the living room, holding Mieko's hand, she felt quite alone, and started closing all the screen doors. "Otoku left me so that I'd be in trouble," she said to herself, realizing that would be difficult for her to go out without someone to take care of Mieko. Then she decided to take the child along, and went to Mieko's chest of drawers to get her ready. She looked for the key, remembering that Otoku had always kept it with her. She found it on top of the chest.

Otoku's sudden disappearance made Komatsu anxious and depressed. She hesitated many times while she helped Mieko change her dress, wondering if she still wanted to go out. It seemed a nuisance now. While she sat by the charcoal brazier, pondering, Mieko came and sat close to her, a blank expression on her face.

"Let's go out anyway," Komatsu said suddenly in a cheerful voice, and she started closing the windows, a chore she had never done before. She locked the front door and walked out to the street. It was getting dark.

Komatsu waited for a while, holding Mieko's hand, and then took a rickshaw to the Nonoses. Kaneko was home, playing cards with her friends.

"Oh, you brought Mieko with you today. That's a surprise," said Kaneko. She had come half way down the staircase, and invited them to come up. Komatsu found familiar faces there.

"Both of them are losing rather desperately. I'm sure they'd welcome a new player," said Kaneko. The older woman was a dowager, the owner of a big, Western-style restaurant in Kyobashi, and the younger one was an old friend of Kaneko's. A kept woman, Komatsu knew. Both of them welcomed Komatsu, while Kaneko took Mieko in her arms and kissed her on the cheek. The other women complimented Mieko on how beautiful and lovely she was.

After she lost three games, Komatsu went downstairs with Mieko to take a break. It was now completely dark outside, and in the kitchen a maid was moving about busily. Komatsu smoked a cigarette and gazed at the hair of her daughter, who sat beside her quietly. She felt very sad, as if she and her daughter were homeless, wandering from one place to another. The strange restlessness and anxiety became so unbearable that she couldn't sit still any longer. Not knowing what else to do, she called Kaneko, who finally came downstairs. Kaneko saw Mieko sitting there, looking bored, and suggested that she have her maid take her home if Komatsu wanted to be alone. She looked at Komatsu's face searchingly.

"To tell the truth, Otoku has left us. So I don't know what to do," said Komatsu.

"Left? What is she thinking, I wonder?"

"She thinks my future is hopeless. She was anxious. The other day I got upset when she complained to me about this and that, and so I said things to her I shouldn't have. That made her feel worse, I'm sure."

"If she's gone, she's gone. But it's inconvenient for you," said Kaneko, keeping her eyes on Komatsu's fair and delicate hands. Komatsu's mind continued to churn with vague anxieties. She stared at Kaneko's face without a word.

"Those women will leave soon. So why don't you make yourself comfortable here and we'll talk about it later," said

Kaneko before going back upstairs. Komatsu was invited to join them again but she didn't feel like playing cards any more. And when Mieko started to fuss, she left the Nonoses with her daughter, heading in the direction of busy streets.

- 4 -

Komatsu walked slowly down the street where the street-cars ran, occasionally stopping to buy cookies and toys for Mieko, but when she realized she couldn't get rid of the child no matter how far she walked, she felt annoyed. She became irritated and wanted to wrench the little hand out of her own. Her irritation turned into a nasty mood that was focused on Mieko, who clung to her mother's index finger as if it were a lifeline. Komatsu felt like pushing her daughter away.

Mieko followed her mother from one brightly lit street to another. Mieko was dressed in an expensive silk crepe kimono with long sleeves and a silk coat over it. But she had neither a cape nor a shawl, and her cheeks, exposed to the cold wind, turned red. Komatsu walked slowly, even slower than her daughter, till she became annoyed at the stares of the people passing by. Then she picked up her pace as if she had remembered that she was walking. Without exception women passersby whispered to each other, and men stared at her rudely. Escaping into a dark, narrow street, Komatsu hurried on, pulling Mieko along by her arm. The child stayed very close to the skirt of her mother's kimono.

"You can stay at your Aunt Kaneko's alone, can't you, Mieko?" Komatsu asked when they came to a stone bridge. It was cold. Mieko didn't say anything and instead looked away into the distance, where a red neon sign blinked on and off. Mieko's silence discouraged Komatsu. Saying no more, she went on walking.

Back at the Nonose house, Komatsu found Kaneko waiting for them. She had been worried.

"You must be tired, Mieko," she said and took her to the charcoal brazier. Kaneko's friends had gone and the house was very quiet. Uneasy, Komatsu went over to the brazier.

"Such a nuisance, that Otoku is. What could she be think-ing?" said Kaneko, picking up the thread of their earlier con-versation as she rubbed Mieko's hands to warm them up. Ko-matsu was agitated and couldn't calm herself. She found it impossible to just sit there looking at Kaneko's face. The dim light made the room look sad. She felt that there was no place where she would be comfortable. She didn't want to think about Otoku.

"Can't you go out tonight?" she asked Kaneko.

"I could if I wanted," Kaneko responded, looking straight at Komatsu. "But where do you want to go?"

"I thought it might be fun to go to the comic theater."

"That sounds good. I'll come with you," said Kaneko, let-ting go of Mieko's hand. "We have to eat first, though. You must be hungry, too."

"We can eat out," said Komatsu. She sounded like she want-ed to leave that moment.

"I'll come, too," said Mieko, who had been listening care-fully to the adults' conversation. She looked worried that she might be left alone.

"Of course we'll take you. Don't worry," said Kaneko as she went to get her portable mirror. "I'll have to comb my hair, though," she said to herself.

"How about you? Would you like to fix your hair?" she asked Komatsu, looking into the mirror and noticing that Ko-matsu was still sitting there. Komatsu didn't want to bother about her hair. It took a long time for Kaneko to get ready. First she had her maid bring hot water with which she tried to straighten her hair, and then she washed her face. Komatsu waited, lost in her own thoughts. Her head, resting on her hands, seemed to be getting heavier.

Komatsu let Mieko and Kaneko go to the theater without her, saying that she would join them shortly. As soon as they left, she took a rickshaw to Chimaki. She couldn't think of anything except seeing Koisaburō. It was only eight o'clock when she got there. Okatsu, one of the maids, came to greet her right away with her usual hospitable smile, and reproached Komatsu for not having come sooner.

"I was worried, thinking you might have been offended the other day," she said, amiably. And then without wasting any time she had the other maid make a phone call to the theater. This maid came back shortly with the message that Koisaburō was unable to come.

"If he can't come, he can't come. There's nothing to do." Komatsu spoke calmly to Okatsu, but unwilling to accept the fact, she lingered.

"It's true he's been ill, but I think there's a woman who is after him, and he can't easily excuse himself. Why don't you wait here for a while. I'll call him myself a bit later," said Okatsu. Then, in order to ease her mind she fussed around, bringing a padded dressing gown made of twilled fabric, which she put over Komatsu's shoulders just in case she was cold. A nice charcoal fire burned inside the *kotatsu* heater, which was covered with a silk comforter. Komatsu told Okatsu that she didn't wish to order any food, and so Okatsu had hot tea and rice crackers brought to her.

"I'll call him again and find out what's going on. Why don't you make yourself comfortable and wait a little while," Okatsu repeated when she left Komatsu. The light shown brightly on the paper sliding doors, which were decorated at the bottom with a black-checkered pattern on silver. Komatsu leaned against a pillar, stretching her legs out inside the comforter. She sat there for a while, alone in the small room, waiting for the answer to the second phone call. Neither Okatsu nor the other maid came back for a long time. Komatsu didn't have the courage to call Okatsu and ask her to hurry. Self-confidence like that belonged to the past, it was like a dream. She continued to sit there, despondent, staring at her knees. Her long eyelashes cast small shadows on her cheeks, and her face wore an expression of nervous irritation. Only when her dark purple coat slipped down from the clothes rack, disturbing the stillness of the room, did she raise her head. Her lovely eyes lowered again when she realized it was only the coat. A deep sigh came from her as she slumped down.

Komatsu couldn't help feeling awkward at Chimaki, where

she had once been a generous patron. The difference between now and days past was all too clear. She had spent her money freely, and even when her financial circumstances began to deteriorate, her vanity demanded that she maintain the same standards. Now her resources were so depleted that it was not even possible to pretend. She felt ashamed that she had to expose herself to the maids at Chimaki in such an inexpensive kimono; she was afraid that they would see through her and pity her. This is the last time I will come here, she said to herself. She felt sad, but knowing that she'd be setting herself free from her obsession, she also experienced a strange sense of relief. In her own mind she had resolved that if Koisaburō wouldn't come to see her that night, she would have to give him up. Still, it was intolerable to be confronted by the shadow of her ruined self. She wished she could be as generous as she used to be, even if it were only while she was at Chimaki. And so she tried to conjure up the memory of the good times she had had with her guests, playing various games with them here in this teahouse. But instead she found her mind assailed by darkness and cold, rising up as if from the bottom of hell. Overwhelmed by her misery, she felt the brilliant world she had once enjoyed, the world in which she had generously treated anyone who would flatter her, was now blocked from her by a thick wall. It all seemed so far away. The other side of the decorative sliding door was filled with glory belonging to someone else now. And Koisaburō, once her own, was surrounded by that splendor. Once her gorgeous sleeves had covered him—her tentative, insecure admirer—like wings. She could see him now in the arms of someone else, doing his best to please the new patron with the same adulation he had shown her. Outside that enclosed, glorious world, the world that was forever lost to her, Komatsu's infatuation remained unquenched. The hopelessness of her affair made Komatsu sad.

"I'll go now," she murmured to herself with a sigh. Her voice lingered, making the room seem even quieter. White chrysanthemums arranged in the vase and placed on the alcove might have trembled at the sound of her voice; their soft shadows on the wall shifted slightly.

"I'll go," she said again, this time more clearly, and kicking off the comforter, got up. She could no longer stay there as a customer, being ignored. She was offended by the mistress, Onao, who had not shown up to greet her. Resolving never to see Koisaburō again, she went to the wall and pressed the bell.

It was Onao who came.

"Madam, I'm so sorry we kept you waiting. What is Okatsu doing, I wonder? But have you really been alone all this time?" said Onao as she entered the room on her knees. She had a thin, oval face, which seemed to have become even thinner and more wrinkled as she got older. Greeting Komatsu in a stiff manner, with her hands pulled into the sleeves of her kimono, she looked like a bird extending and folding her wings. With her hair done up and the collar of her kimono pulled back, her back looked more rounded than it really was. She must have been with her customers. Her cheeks were flushed and her lips had the luster of wine, now dried.

"The line was busy and we were able to get through only a few minutes ago, you see. As I thought, Koisaburō's been ill. He's been pushing himself because he doesn't want to miss any of his performances, he says. I told him you waited the other day too, and that he should at least make an appearance, you know. But he's like a spoiled child when he's not well, and he wouldn't listen to me at all," Onao said with a little laugh.

"Thank you all for your trouble," said Komatsu, getting ready to leave.

"I really don't like letting you go like this. We'll let you know when he can see you as soon as he gets well."

"I'll see you later," responded Komatsu, regaining her calm expression as she left Chimaki.

- 5 -

Although the hood was up, it was cold in the rickshaw. Komatsu's body, stiff and frozen from the sharp sting of the cold air, was not easily warmed. Trembling in the rickshaw, she bit her lips and held her breath. The chill seemed to spread from her chilled lips to her entire body, even though she covered her lips with her long velvet scarf. She pulled to her neck the quilted gown the mistress of Chimaki had thrown over on her shoulders and held it tightly.

The pale violet moon cast shadows across the frozen ground, the frost glittering in its light. Occasionally the street lamps shot their long straight beams of light into her eyes, making the ground look like the surface of water. The frost seemed to penetrate the rickshaw as it moved along quietly. Looking at the cold, dreary scene of the winter night through the rickshaw's small viewing window on the front cover, and seeing the gloomy streets stretching beyond her endlessly, Komatsu felt depressed and slightly irritated. The rickshaw seemed to be slowly sinking through a lightless underworld; from time to time the scene in front of her turned pitch dark from the layers of shadows that piled on top of one another. She wondered where she was and tried to remember the route from Chimaki in Tsukiji to Akasaka, where she lived. She had taken the rickshaw along the same route several times before but could not remember whether she had ever gone through streets this dark.

The rickshaw was now crossing a bridge. Closing her eyes and leaning her head against the back of the seat, Komatsu tried not to look out at the dark city. The rickshaw swayed a little once in a while; her skin no longer felt the sting of the cold. An image of indulgence, soaked in crimson, appeared in the weary darkness behind her closed eyes. Slowly the image became clearer, and in its center was Koisaburō, standing still and looking resplendent in red and purple. He was looking at her and his eyes were filled with innocent yearning. He gazed persistently at Komatsu, trying to lure her into a love that was not illusory.

A cold blast of air on her smooth skin brought Komatsu back to reality; the sensation resembled, somehow, that of her dream world. She opened her eyes, which seemed glued together, and was momentarily blinded by the bright lights of the outside world. She stared at the street lamps for a moment, puzzled, then sank back into the intoxication of her fantasy world. She let herself imagine that she was sitting in the rickshaw with Koisaburō. She even thought she heard a rustling sound from the lining of his overcoat.

Komatsu wondered why she hadn't phoned Koisaburō herself when she was at Chimaki. She regretted it. If she had spoken to him and asked him directly, he couldn't have declined, out of mere courtesy to her. She was sorry she had restrained herself, but she had feared she would be seen as an obstinate, inexperienced woman, and had therefore left the matter in the hands of the Chimaki mistress. She now felt she must listen to Koisaburō's voice once more, even on the phone. This new idea made her suddenly impatient. Unable to sit still any longer, she called to the rickshaw man.

"I wonder if you can find a public phone somewhere around here?" she said, flushed.

The young man stopped running and paused for a few moments, thinking. He then turned back the way he had come, and took a narrow, dark street. Halfway up the street, however, he seemed to realize that he had made a mistake. He looked out across the street and turned around, mumbling something to himself. Komatsu realized now that they were near Shimbashi. The rickshaw proceeded on this willow-lined street for a while and crossed to the other side to make another turn. There he found a small, lighted phone booth.

Komatsu called Koisaburō's home first and was told that he was not expected back that night. Disappointed, she called the theater teahouse, where she had also been a patron. When she said she wanted to know about Koisaburō's illness, the mistress of the teahouse came on the line and said that Koisaburō was ill and seemed to have gone home early, leaving his last performance to the substitute.

"I wish you had called a bit earlier. Did you make an arrangement to see him tonight?" the mistress asked in a low voice, slowly. Remembering it was at this teahouse that her affair with Koisaburō had started, Komatsu felt she was listening to the voice of an old friend whom she hadn't seen for a long time. As she left the phone she was filled with nostalgic sweetness.

There was nothing to do but give up. Once again under the cover of the rickshaw, she saw the handsome face of her fickle lover come and go. "There's someone after him"—she repeated the words of the Chimaki maid, and thought about the woman who now was Koisaburō's lover. She envisioned his half-naked body on the lap of this other woman—the body that once lay next to her with his head resting in her lap. She felt a great fatigue and a cruel sadness all at once; it was as if some unknown force had overtaken her and pushed her away. She was defeated. The thought that she had been expelled from the world of glory tormented her.

Koisaburō's eyebrows, painted with black and red, which showed just a little at the edge where the brush swept up; his eyes with their clear outline, nicely slanted; the way he focused those gentle, alluring eyes under his long eyelashes, so lovely, so charming. . . . Komatsu went on composing the picture of her lover. At the end she said to herself that surely she would never see him again. She no longer felt sad, but weary and resigned. She no longer wanted to join her daughter and Kaneko at the comic theater. Instead, she wanted to do something exciting, something that would clear her mind. She finally hit upon the idea of buying something nice and having it sent to Koisaburō. When she thought of having it delivered to his house so that it would be waiting for him, she smiled as if a flower had suddenly opened in her heart.

She ordered the rickshaw to go back to Ginza and had the man wait at a corner while she walked and looked into the stores along the street. She looked up at a clock tower stretching high into the dark sky and saw that it was ten minutes till eleven. Most of the stores were closed, and she couldn't find anything that satisfied her. She gave up and went back to the rickshaw, stumbling along like a drunkard and feeling a nagging headache.

From Ginza she went straight back to Kaneko's house, where she found that Kaneko had already returned.

"Mieko cried and wouldn't stop. So we came back, leaving a message at the theater for you. She fell asleep, finally, a little

while ago," said Kaneko who sat by the charcoal brazier, looking sullen.

Original title: *Eiga* (1916).

Miyamoto Yuriko

(1899–1951)

WHILE MANY JAPANESE WRITERS fell silent or wrote harmless material, if not military propaganda, during the late 1930s, Miyamoto Yuriko remained determined to express her belief in communism and the liberation of women in her writing. She was one of the few writers of this period who held firm to her radical views, despite great pressure and physical torture by authorities. With the close of World War II, Yuriko emerged as a leader of the intellectuals, and her literary career had followed a long and dramatic course that was rare among Japanese women writers.

Although most of Yuriko's major works of fiction are auto-biographical, they do not tend to focus on the awakening of a female protagonist within the confinement of the family institution, a subject explored by many women writers of the previous generation. Her themes reflect the turbulent times in which she wrote, and her heroines' social and political concerns as well as their inner struggles are carefully examined. In this sense, and in the breadth of her intellectual and emotional experiences, Yuriko might be compared with Simone de Beauvoir: As a feminist and as a writer, Yuriko, like de Beauvoir, challenged the institutions and mores of the middle-class milieu into which she was born and about which she wrote in her fiction.

Yuriko was only seventeen years old when she became a celebrated writer overnight with the publication of a novella, *A Flock of Poor People* (*Mazushii Hitobito no Mure*) in the prestigious magazine, *Central Forum* (*Chūō Kōron*). Her auspicious start was encouraged by her parents—a loving, understanding father who was a successful architect, and a strong-willed, passionate mother who was from the family of a prominent educator. Her mother, in fact, helped to successfully promote the publication of *A Flock of Poor People*. A precocious child, Yuriko had begun writing stories for her own enjoyment at the age of seven or so. In high school she found her studies unexciting and spent a great deal of time in the public library, reading Edgar Allan Poe and Oscar Wilde, or simply sitting in the open field all day. Along with translating various Japanese classics into the modern language and binding her versions into hand-made books, she wrote sentimental love stories. She soon discovered Russian novels, and was particularly drawn to the work of Tolstoy.

Another early influence, which remained a source of inspiration throughout her writing career, was closer to home: a small village her grandfather helped to develop and a place to which she returned many times in later years to retreat and to write. This village was the model for *A Flock of Poor People*, which sympathetically portrayed the poor farmers of the village and the crippling effects of poverty. Yuriko's deep concern for nameless people and her belief in the inherent goodness of humankind remained strong throughout her life, supporting her through many hardships.

Yuriko's development as a writer was also shaped by the common struggles shared by women of her generation. Before she could tackle the task of gender liberation, however, she had to deal with another, more immediate problem, that of freeing herself from her overprotective parents and from their middle-class conventions. In 1919, twenty years old and in New York City, thousands of miles from home, Yuriko openly defied her parents and married a man who did not meet with their approval. Yuriko had decided to go to New York on the spur of the moment, perhaps because she was bored at the Japan Women's College, perhaps because she needed to escape from the pressure to follow up on her acclaimed writing debut. She enrolled as an auditor at Columbia University, where she met her husband, a perennial graduate student fifteen years her senior who was majoring in Near Eastern languages. The newly married couple returned to Japan when Yuriko's mother fell ill; they lived for a while in Yuriko's parents' house till her husband found a teaching job and they eventually were able to move to their own place.

After five years of marriage, which were filled with conflict and pain, Yuriko divorced her husband. Motivated by a desire to re-examine past choices and to make sense of her failed relationship, Yuriko had begun writing an autobiographical novel. The first chapter of *Nobuko* appeared in *Central Forum* in the summer of 1924, but it would be three years before the novel was completed.

Some months before this first chapter was published, Nogami Yaeko, a friend and established writer, introduced Yuriko to Yuasa Yoshiko, a journalist and scholar of Russian literature. Yoshiko was to have a profound influence on Yuriko. A unique friendship immediately sprang up between the two women; Yuriko was strongly attracted to Yoshiko's personality, which was very different from her own, and by the fact that she led a life defiant of middle-class institutions such as marriage. Yoshiko, who was a lesbian, became a source of inspiration and encouragement for Yuriko, both to continue her work on *Nobuko* and to take the final step towards divorce.

Nobuko is a record of the familial and internal battles that Yuriko fought as a young woman, and it is her best and most widely read novel. At one point the heroine of the story declares that she must escape from a marriage she had entered to escape her overbearing family, closely paralleling Yuriko's own struggle and her decisive move to end a relationship she later likened to "being bogged down in mud." Yuriko's divorce was a move to freedom, and her relationship with Yoshiko helped her fulfill a desire to grow and expand her horizons.

Yuriko and Yoshiko shared each other's lives for seven years. During the first few, they lived together in a large rented house and led a relatively uneventful life, which is described in Yuriko's novella, *One Flower*, (*Ippon no Hana*), 1927. At the end of 1927, Yoshiko made plans to go to the Soviet Union in order to polish her Russian, and Yuriko decided at the last minute to accompany her. Yuriko spent three years touring the Soviet Union as well as several Western cities, an experience that was to change her life.

Inspired by the revolutionary society in the Soviet Union and appalled by the poverty she witnessed in Western cities, Yuriko returned to Japan in 1930 an avowed Marxist. She wrote many reports and essays about the people of the Soviet Union, particularly about the active role women played in the revolutionary movement. During the 1920s it was fashionable for Japanese writers to take up socialist themes in their books and to participate in left-wing politics, and Yuriko was one of many intellectuals that supported radical causes, even before she traveled to the Soviet Union. But Yuriko's commitment was serious and deep-rooted, and she spent the rest of her life as a tireless crusader for the communist movement and for the autonomy of women. Many of her works deal with both women's concerns and class issues; among the best is "The Breast" (*Chibusa*), a story about a day care worker's awakening to revolutionary consciousness through her involvement with a city traffic workers' strike.

Yuriko joined the Japan Leftist Writers Alliance and in 1930 she was made coordinator of the Women's Committee of the All-Japan Artists Association and chief editor of their journal, *Working Woman* (*Hataraku Fujin*). Through these various activities she met Miyamoto Kenji, a leftist critic and member of the Japanese Communist Party, who was to become her second husband. Yuriko's marriage to this charismatic man nine years her junior brought to an end her relationship with Yuasa Yoshiko. Years later in her autobiographical novel, *Signpost* (*Dōhyō*), Yuriko would write about her relationship with Yoshiko.

In the early 1930s police intervention in leftist activities became fierce, and a few months after their marriage, Kenji went underground in order to escape arrest. The police were not aware of Yuriko's Party membership, but even so she was arrested and held in detention on several occasions, which resulted in the deterioration of her health. She consistently refused to disavow her political beliefs, and consequently all publication of her work was effectively censored by magazine and book publishers, in cooperation with the military government.

Ultimately Kenji was arrested and sentenced to life imprisonment. These were difficult years for Yuriko. Her parents died during this period, leaving her with no source of income. When Yuriko was not under arrest, she cared for Kenji's aged parents, studied the history of Japanese women writers, and attended court hearings where Kenji was being tried for being a Communist. During his imprisonment, Yuriko officially changed her name from Chūjō Yuriko to Miyamoto Yuriko, as a birthday present to Kenji.

Not until the conclusion of World War II were Yuriko and Kenji reunited. During the war years, Yuriko had been working on manuscripts, gathering information and writing about the cruel treatment she and her comrades had received at the hands of the police. The experiences of these individuals, their sufferings and their joyous celebrations when the country was finally liberated from military oppression, are masterfully rendered in the two novels, *The Banshu Plain* (*Banshū Heiya*)and *Weather Vane Grasses* (*Fūchisō*).

During the following year, Yuriko put the finishing touches on a novel that takes up where she had left off in *Nobuko*. This work, entitled *Two Gardens*, along with her next major novel, *Signpost*, completed her autobiographical trilogy. The works bear witness to a woman's struggle for personal freedom and growth and her developing political consciousness. Considered her most significant fiction, the novels of this trilogy are also particularly important for illuminating Yuriko's concerns as a woman and an artist.

Yuriko never fully regained her physical health following her years of imprisonment, and she died suddenly at age fifty-two, at the height of her creative power. At the time of her death she was widely regarded as the conscience of the intellectuals and a writer deeply concerned with the condition of Japanese women. A writer devoted to her personal relationships and political commitments as well as to her art, she is remembered today both for her written works and her lifetime of political activism.

Y. T.

Nobuko

translated by Yukiko Tanaka

Chapter III (4)

Nobuko felt she had changed. Tsukuda was constantly on her mind, and this affected her day to day life. Her parents were uncertain about the match, and could not relate to their daughter in the same way as they had before.

As the days went by Nobuko was able to see why her mother was confused and upset about Tsukuda, particularly in view of all the circumstances. What Takeyo had read in her daughter's letters, and what she had heard from her husband, were quite different from what she had learned from the newspaper and other sources. Takeyo had not yet met Tsukuda, so it was inevitable that she would mistrust him. She had no way of knowing which reports were accurate, but she did know that her daughter was naive and her husband easygoing and she therefore felt justified in imagining whatever she wanted about Tsukuda. Still, Nobuko was suspicious of her mother's tendency to be overly cautious, ever paranoid, toward any man who approached Nobuko, assuming his intentions to be evil. Nobuko felt indignant on Tsukuda's behalf because she knew that his poverty and lack of favorable connections had greatly contributed to her mother's poor opinion of him.

Her daughter's return had been a great satisfaction to Takeyo, of course, and whenever the two sat down together Takeyo couldn't help telling her daughter how lonely she had been while Nobuko was away. But inevitably, their conversation would turn to Tsukuda and as soon as his name was mentioned, Takeyo would lose her composure. The long hours after her father left for work were trying ones for Nobuko.

"Nobuko," Takeyo called out one day from the living room. Nobuko, in her room, heard her and felt a vague annoyance. She stood up and went to her mother, however.

"What is it?" she asked as she opened the sliding door.

Takeyo had books of color samples open on her lap. "Kikuya was here," she answered, holding the color samples up toward the paper screen so that she could see them in a better light.

"What are you going to dye?"

"I have some silk that I can dye and have it made into a *haori* jacket. It's hard to find a color I like nowadays. I wonder if it's because of poor dyestuffs," said Takeyo. "What happened to the purple silk kimono you took along?" she asked abruptly, as if she'd suddenly remembered something.

"I still have it."

"I don't think you can wear it now. It's got such a nice pattern, though."

Still half-preoccupied with color selection, she continued, "What are you going to do about your kimonos? You have to have a few new ones, at least."

"I'm not interested. Besides, I don't need any.

"You can't just say that. . . . Well, in any case, let's decide on this," Takeyo said and handed the silk and the color samples to the maid.

"What sort of place is the province where Mr. Tsukuda is from, I wonder," she said after a while as she was closing the wardrobe. Her mind seemed to make an obvious connection between the two.

"I don't know . . . but why do you ask? I've never been there, you know."

"It seems rather strange. Now that you're back in Japan, I would expect someone come to visit, even though it's only for formality's sake. Or perhaps Mr. Tsukuda hasn't told his family yet. Is that it?"

"Oh, yes, he has told them."

"Then does that mean they're waiting for the bride's family to come to them first?" Takeyo's voice was full of irony and hurt pride.

"They probably can't think of what to say. That's why they haven't come, I'm sure. When Tsukuda gets back, they'll do whatever's appropriate," said Nobuko indifferently, not knowing how else to respond. This, however, annoyed Takeyo.

"You and your husband may find nothing wrong with it. After all, you're not like the rest of us," she said and closed the wardrobe, clanging the metal handle. "But, as I've been thinking, you ought to know that your doing things differently from other people doesn't necesarily mean you are right. It annoys people when you act eccentric," she continued.

"I am not eccentric. You and I have different personalities— we think differently. That's all."

"Do you believe, then, that you're always right in everything you do?"

There were many occasions when mother and daughter got into heated arguments. Nobuko tried to stay calm, but Takeyo's intense and relentless carping would in the end force her to lose her control. When she was worked up, she revealed the same strong, unyielding nature as her mother.

"It seems we've been repeating the same things ever since I returned. Let's stop, all right? I know what you think, but I don't want to keep talking like this," said Nobuko one day toward the end of January, when she found herself in yet another volatile conversation with her mother.

"You've changed. You never said things like that before," Takeyo responded in an argumentative voice. Her cheeks were flushed. "You used to be sincere and good-hearted. You were willing to talk things out; in fact, that was your strength. I don't know whose influence it is, but you certainly have changed."

Nobuko felt agitated, as if her heart had been stabbed and was now being stirred with a small pointed object. Takeyo knew just how to inject a poisonous needle into the most vulnerable spot of Nobuko's heart; she had a woman's instinct toward another woman, and a mother's toward her daughter. She nearly always succeeded in getting a rise out of Nobuko. Today, however, Nobuko was able to remain calm.

"I'm not avoiding discussion for selfish reasons. We shouldn't argue just for the sake of argument—that's all I'm saying."

"That's what I call selfish. You did what you wanted, you threw mud in your parents' faces. Then you tell me to be calm and reasonable. You don't have the right to talk to me like that. To what end have I gone through all this pain for you, even sending you abroad? You think about that," said Takeyo, now crying. Her mother raised her hand to dry her tears, and Nobuko saw the fingers that revealed her advancing age. She felt wretched. She got up from her chair and went to her.

"Mother, why don't you stop thinking about Tsukuda? And then ask yourself if there's even one man among those you know who you think would be right for me to fall in love with. Have you ever wanted me to have a relationship with a man—any man—who came into my life? The answer is 'No,' isn't it? No matter who he was, you thought he was worthless as soon as I showed a real interest in him," Nobuko said, trying to both comfort her mother and make herself understood.

"If I'm a wicked old woman, then. . . ," began Takeyo, offended.

"That's not what I meant, Mother," Nobuko said, putting her hand on Takeyo's and trying to prevent her from turning her face away. "I'm trying to be objective. Your expectations are too high. You're an idealist when it concerns me. Don't you see? Surely you're aware of how much you have hoped for me, my work and my success. You're trying to make me do what you couldn't do with your own life. Isn't that right?"

"You may be right there." Takeyo was no longer angry.

"I know I am right. You'd like to see me as your girl, pure and lofty, transcending such things as love affairs."

"I'm not saying you should remain single. I've always thought I'd be happy to see you married to a fine man, who could enlighten you."

"The reasons for getting married . . . are probably different for you and me."

"You don't have to tell me that. I know," snapped Takeyo, once again assuming a severe tone. "You talk like a Bolshevik."

"What most girls want is to get married, settle down, and do things in exactly the same manner as their husbands. They want to live as stable a life as they can. That's why they choose a partner from their own class, someone who grew up with similar values; or someone from a slightly higher or much higher class, if that's their fate. I'm different. I'm not a bit interested in having a man who grew up just like I did, who has seen only what I've seen, and who has parents just like you and Father. I'd feel uneasy with that. I'm drawn to a man who is different from . . . I wonder if you understand me? Tsukuda's good and bad points aside, I don't think you'd be satisfied with any choice I make. I am a bit like a savage, you see, and so I won't be happy unless I can grab what I want with my own hands."

Nobuko stopped. Takeyo did not say anything. The two sat there in silence for quite a while, gazing at the flames in the fireplace that gleamed in the approaching dusk.

Chapter IV (3)

They received no visitors in their home. Perhaps because he had not received his higher education in Japan, Tsukuda had very few friends.

Tsukuda went for walks quite often, and Nobuko went with him. On a few occasions they bought seedlings of Chinese black pine and white cedar, and later planted them by the cliff on the west side of the house as well as by the gate. Their neighborhood, crowded with small houses, had hardly any space for trees, though one could see in the distance the tips of the trees on Koishikawa Hill. The Chinese black pines with their bright green needles caught the attention of the neighborhood children, and after school several of them would gather around the seedlings.

"Hey, do you know what kind of tree this is?"

"A pine."

"No, it's not. It's not a pine. Pines have prickly needles."

"Hey, look what you've done!" One of them shouted a few minutes later.

"They'll be mad," said another timid voice.

When Tsukuda was home during these visits Nobuko couldn't help getting depressed. When he heard the children's voices, he became tense, responding to them as if they were adults. He picked up his clogs and quietly went to the garden, crossed to the side door attached to the fence, and unlatched the gate without making a noise, suddenly appearing before the children. His soundless appearance sent the children running. Nobuko could tell how scared they were by the sound of their fading footsteps. After this had happened more than a few times, she began feeling sad and miserable.

"Such a nuisance," she said. "Trees are rare around here, that's why. We'd better transplant them inside the fence."

"It's inexcusable. Picking the branches of other people's trees. But I won't transplant them. Never." Nobuko sensed in her husband's words a stubborn attachment to possessions.

She would have preferred to buy books rather than seedlings. They often stopped at a used bookstore, where she would pick up books and show them to her husband.

"Do you have to have this?" he would ask, examining the book carefully.

She was discouraged by the tone of his voice. She would put the book back on the shelf, saying that she could wait. She knew she wouldn't feel good if she insisted on getting it; she would be no happier than if she didn't have it. She realized, after living with him for a while, that Tsukuda had not learned to overcome the disadvantages of a childhood spent in poverty; he couldn't get comfortable with poverty, control it, be bold—even cheerful—about it.

Nobuko spent most of her days at home, reading and listening to the women talking by the well down at the bottom of the cliff. The time passed slowly. She waited eagerly for Tsukuda's return, and as soon as he got home she wanted to pour herself out, let the dam inside her break; she wanted him to talk, too. He didn't seem to find the things she wanted to talk about particularly interesting and showed very little enthusiasm. What he was eager to talk about was what went on at work, mainly gossip about his colleagues.

"I had to see the chief quite a few times today," he told Nobuko one evening in a low voice, as if he were telling a secret, "and Tsutsumi asked me, whispering, if I had something important to discuss with the chief."

"Oh? And?"

"I simply told him that I needed to consult with him. They're all so nervous, you know. I bet I shock them because whenever I want to, I go ahead and talk to the chief, or anyone else for that matter." He sounded proud of himself.

"Sounds like a Gogol story, doesn't it?" said Nobuko, but then she realized that Tsukuda himself was obviously one of those petty officials. It was depressing.

It was far into fall and the moon shone brightly on their garden and onto the roofs crowded together beneath the cliff. Crickets chirped under the floor. On the cold mornings after the first frost, Nobuko could hear from her bed the clopping sound of the clogs worn by the factory workers as they walked along the frozen road as early as six in the morning.

She felt that sorrow had slowly settled in her heart like a sediment. She felt dissatisfied every day, all day long. The absence of stimulation, of an atmosphere that would nurture her artistic sensibility, tortured her. Perhaps she didn't have a great talent, but still, she wished to cultivate her mind and soul and for that a nurturing atmosphere was as essential as food for the body.

Having been around American women for many years, Tsukuda didn't mind if Nobuko stayed in bed till late in the morning. He did the daily shopping willingly, and even helped with the cooking. Her head clear after a good night's sleep, Nobuko devoured her books, absorbing them like a sponge, but what good was that if she couldn't share it with anyone? Tsukuda seemed to have unloaded most of the spirtual burden he used to carry once the routine of his daily life was well established. His intellectual reservoir did not seem to be expanding beyond what he had acquired as a student. He now subscribed to only one literary magazine. And yet he had the skill of an experienced teacher in dodging Nobuko's verbal attacks. But how humiliating and hopeless, she thought. Occasionally she burst into tears, unable to contain her sense of desolation.

"Why do I feel so lonely? Why lonely? We have to do something, anything," she would say.

Perplexed, Tsukuda would knit his eyebrows and embrace her. "Don't cry, please. Things will get better. Soon you'll get used to. . . ," he would say softly again and again, stroking her back, soothingly.

"Getting used to" was exactly what Nobuko feared. It was sad and horrifying that a human being would sooner or later become used to his environment, like a domestic animal. Would I eventually get used to this existence, she wondered. Would I lose my interest and passion for life and become a person far different from what I had once wanted to become? And if so, would I end my life without realizing what I had lost? She mourned for the days that were already lost, and suffered from deep anxiety.

One day in March, Nobuko went to Dōzaka. Her parents' house was lively with visiting relatives and their children. Kazuichirō took photos of everybody.

"The light's good today," he said to Nobuko. "Shall I take another picture of you alone?"

"I suppose. . . ." she said. Nobuko didn't like to have pictures taken by professional photographers but felt intrigued by her brother's offer. She was curious to see how she looked. "I'd like a picture, but don't let it come out blurred, making me look like a ghost."

"Don't worry. I won't botch it on a clear day like this," Kazuichirō said. Nobuko went out to the yard with her brother and posed by a devilwood.

Several days later when she went to Dōzaka again, the photos were ready.

"I think they should be dry now," Kazuichirō said and Nobuko followed him to the darkroom he had partitioned off at
the back of the laundry room. By the window near several
bottles of chemicals, hung the negatives.

"My, there are a lot of pictures. Did you take all of them the
other day?"

"No. Some I took later, when I went to the school with
Tsuyako. There was some film left in the camera."

"Let me see those," said Nobuko.

"This one I took at the school." The picture must have been
taken when Tsuyako was not expecting it. She was talking to
her brother, and laughing; her limbs were nicely stretched,
moving with a rhythmic grace.

"These are from the other day. Moto moved and so they're
a little blurred. The one I took of you alone is better," said
Kazuichirō, handing a sepia-colored photo to Nobuko. It was
developed nicely and the person in the picture was certainly
herself, but the moment she saw it she had the strange sensation that the woman standing by the devilwood tree was
someone else. A strange expression that she didn't recognize
was on the face looking out at her. Do I have these vertical
lines above my eyebrows? It was a complex face, severe—the
face of a person older than she was. A faint, forced smile twisted around the mouth. Altogether an ugly face.

Do I really look like this? she asked herself silently as she
gazed at the picture.

"It could be a bit darker. I'll develop another one for you,"
said Kazuichirō, who mistook Nobuko's silence for a sign of
dissatisfaction with the way the picture came out.

"Oh, no. This is fine. Thank you," said Nobuko, looking at
the picture again. "It's nicely done."

Chapter V (5)

The visit of the Crown Prince of England had stirred up a great
deal of excitement among the public. A large welcome gate

had been erected at Babasaki and people walked along the
moat under brightly lit arc lamps and pine tree branches—
which somehow looked different. Tsukuda's father had been
enjoying the festive streets of the capital, and now he had returned home with various practical souvenirs.

After the old man left, the nights seemed longer. With the
windows open at night the fragrance of spring, of soil and of
new foliage, came drifting into the room. One such evening
Tsukuda was busy opening packages that had arrived from
abroad. Nobuko sat next to him collecting the discarded papers and strings. The only sound in the quiet room was of
coarse paper being folded.

"Would you please go and get the invoice from my desk,
dear?" Tsukuda said. Nobuko did as she was asked, and Tsukuda started checking the books now piled up on the table
against the invoice.

". . . Honey," Nobuko had been watching her husband and
now she spoke with a sense of urgency. But Tsukuda, absorbed in what he was doing, didn't seem to notice.

"What is it, dear?" he answered absently.

"I have something to discuss."

"What is it?"

"Tell me, are all couples like us? Is there no other way?"

"Well, I don't know what you mean exactly, but I suppose
so."

"Can't we be freer?"

"Why? Are you saying you want to live some other way?"
Tsukuda looked at Nobuko's face cautiously, picking up a
book as he spoke.

"I . . . I've been thinking for some time that maybe we
should separate for a while."

"I see no need for that." His tone was sharp, as if he wanted
to cut her off.

"But I'd like to discuss it with you. I've been wanting to for
some time, but I thought I'd wait till your father left."

Nobuko had thought more than once that separation might
be the solution. The more she thought, the more she became
convinced that it was the only way to explore the possibility of

making a new life for herself. She had learned from living with Tsukuda that arguing with him about their differences would bring no change whatsoever in their day to day life. He was not that type of person; he was stubborn in his unique, passive way.

It was impossible, Nobuko thought, to live with him and yet not to come under his influence. Being his accomplice, simply because he was her husband, and feeling uncomfortable about the way she lived, was more than she could endure. In trying not to be lured into his way of thinking Nobuko became over-critical. Looking at her husband with these eyes, she saw, so clearly and ruthlessly, that the man standing in front of her was living a life antithetical to her own.

And that man was her husband! I sleep with this man, but I can't find in our relationship the pure love one ought to feel toward one's marriage partner—my enthusiasm for life, my hope, everything I need to sustain myself, are gone, she thought.

Furthermore, now that Nobuko couldn't trust Tsukuda's sincerity, the agreement to be wife and husband had lost its authority. If they lived their lives independent of each other and disregarded the formality of marriage, both of them would feel more comfortable, more natural, she was sure. Having thought it through, Nobuko suggested the idea, knowing that Tsukuda would object.

"It's unusual, I know, but if we got sick, we'd go somewhere for a change of air, or to the hospital. In our case, the marriage is in need of treatment."

"I don't understand you, dear. As I have said more than once, you are free. You have total freedom and can do whatever you feel like. I, for myself, cannot consent to such a proposal," said Tsukuda. Two deep lines appeared on his forehead as always when he was confronted with issues he'd rather avoid.

Nobuko went on, trying to clarify her thinking to him. She said that she wouldn't go back to her parents' house at Dōzaka after the separation, and that he would not be financially responsible for her.

"Our life together has been strange—false—and I thought

at least a part of it would be cleared up if we each started over again, living a life faithful to our own nature. Don't you agree? We are deceiving ourselves, and that's harmful."

"What sin have we committed?" Tsukuda asked. He looked at Nobuko with the startled eyes of a person who'd been slapped in the face. "I live my life with a pure heart, and *I* love *you*. I don't fear being summoned to stand before God at any time."

"That's not what I mean by false. Let me explain, we. . . ." She hesitated for a moment as if frightened by what she was going to say. She spoke quickly. "We've been secretly disagreeing with each other for a long time; you know that. And yet you keep pretending not to notice anything until I bring it up. Why? I don't . . . like you when you're like that, I find you aggravating. What's worse is that recently I feel I can't talk to you about my problems. I feel we're deadlocked. Besides, I think it's odious to go on acting as if we're a fine couple when in fact we're quite muddled."

"I am sorry that you are so unhappy, even though I love you and I'm devoted to you. But I can't agree to a separation. Never," said Tsukuda in a strained voice. He had put his books away, folded his arms across his chest. His lips quivered a little. Nobuko felt embarrassed and skeptical as she listened to her husband freely use such words as pure and love.

"Why do you think you can't?" she said. "We'd be married still, only trying it over as beginners, that's all."

"Impossible! You must think of my situation. As a teacher I cannot possibly do such a thing. I wouldn't be able to face my colleagues again. People do think we're an ideal couple, you know."

"That doesn't sound right," Nobuko said eagerly. "I don't agree with what you're saying. First of all, we can't live worrying about what people think of us. You say you can't face them again, but as I see it that is where we let each other down. If, in fact, there's something one might call 'ideal' in our relationship, then that's all the more reason to disregard appearances and do whatever possible to enrich ourselves. Don't you agree? We don't want to live like most couples and just sit around."

Tsukuda did not respond for some time. Then he said in an unexpectedly calm voice, almost compassionately, "Are you really convinced that our relationship would improve if we lived apart for a while?"

Nobuko couldn't say that she was convinced. It might be better, or it might not. But, if a separation would enable them to live more naturally, she thought it would do them good. She wanted to clean up the marriage, get rid of the clutter— the habits, the unenlightened ideas, all those sorts of things. To keep on feeling antagonistic, even hateful, toward Tsukuda because she was imprisoned in the relationship, was unbearable, not only for herself but for Tsukuda, too.

In Tsukuda's opinion, however, couples were to stay together, especially if there was some basic disagreement. A couple should correct each other's problems through their life together, that's what a marriage partner was for.

Listening to her husband defending his position infuriated Nobuko. She looked as if she might attack him; her face turned pale.

"You have never, even once, responded to me straightforwardly, like a man. Have you ever admitted, even to yourself, that you were wrong?" She stared at her husband; tears poured from her eyes. "This is what I call hell. You are either indifferent or cunning. When I get upset and say or do something rude and then apologize, you think I've taken back what I said. You go on as if nothing's happened. Your words are empty. You can't say you live your life sincerely." She wiped her tears with her sleeve. "I'm a fool, and so I've said to myself, 'Maybe next time,' so many times. But I can't go on like this any longer!"

"I want you to believe in my sincerity," Tsukuda said, knitting his eyebrows and shaking his head as if he were deeply grieved.

"But I don't believe it. I can't . . . any longer."

"I can see that . . . Otherwise you wouldn't say things like. . . ."

After a few minutes of silence, which seemed like an hour to Nobuko, he asked, "You really want to separate, then?"

His voice wavered, startling Nobuko and she looked up at

her husband. He turned his pale, tired face away from her, waiting for her response. She felt that her answer would have fatal consequences.

"I just think it would be better." Her voice was heavy, like feet dragging through the mud.

When he heard this, Tsukuda made a small gesture as if to indicate that he had reached his conclusion. "Well, that's it, then. If we can't live together, we should divorce," he said. Nobuko did not respond.

"Is that all right? I don't think there's any other way. I will go back to my home in the country. I must say I truly regret that this happened. I am really sorry, but I can't help it," he added, looking at Nobuko, who remained quiet, her chin in her hand, her elbow propped on the armrest of the chair. Nobuko felt that she was about to take another step, guided by some unknown force.

"You're saying something different now," she said.

"Why? Why different? For me it's all the same. . . . I know you don't understand the first thing about me. If you believe what you've been saying. . . ." And then suddenly he grabbed her hands and pulled them to his head. He started crying and tore at his hair with his hands, which were still holding hers. "Why haven't we stayed friends?"

Chapter VI (6)

A distorted, pale face wet with tears; hair matted on his forehead like a drowned person's; his voice—remembering the scene of a few days ago, Nobuko shuddered. A peculiar uneasiness stayed with her. It was as though she'd had a glimpse of some dreadful truth. But she also felt like she'd been watching a stage performance. Some time ago, when Tsukuda had shown tears in a sentimental display in front of her parents, he had cast strong doubts in Nobuko's mind about his sincerity. Men did not cry unless they had a very good reason, she had always thought; their tears were more sincere than women's, she had believed.

She looked at the out-of-season primroses that Tsukuda had left for her in a glass on her desk. They impressed her as his tears had. The small, pale pink flowers had bloomed from a cluster of roots the previous resident of the house had left by the backyard fence. The tiny flowers on the desk seemed to be saying something to her. Torn between opposing emotions— she did not want to look at the flowers, yet guilt prevented her from throwing them away—Nobuko gazed at them for a long time. She felt Tsukuda's tight grasp all over her body as if she were bound with wire. Whatever his real reason was, he didn't want me to go, he wanted to keep me as his possession.

Nobuko was able to see why Tsukuda might feel distressed. Since their marriage, it was she who had acted selfishly. At least in most people's eyes it wasn't he who had taken undue advantage. She had gone on trips by herself, she had stayed in bed late in the morning. And yet, she couldn't help feeling annoyed at the notion that those small freedoms were granted to her because she was his legitimate wife. It was disheartening to see her husband assume she was content on the basis of these insignificant freedoms. Her heart suffered from loneliness because Tsukuda stopped at this point. More than anything else, she sensed his desire to show the world that he truly loved her. There had been unfair criticism about their marriage: that he married Nobuko not out of love but to gain social status. It would be painful for him to give credence to this criticism through separation; it would show him a failure. He wanted to maintain, if only for the sake of appearances, that their marriage was successful, to show the world how wrong it had been. He wanted to prove, even belatedly, that their marriage was based on genuine love. To Nobuko his motivation was impure. What she sensed in him was the obstinance of a pragmatic middle-aged man who did not want any disruptions in the status quo. It was only in this secondary motive that Nobuko found him sincere. He was not moved by love, that emotion not easily grasped, but something always light and warm and nurturing for those who experience it.

Whenever she had a chance, Nobuko tried to get back to the

issue of separation, which somehow had been dropped, unresolved.

"I wonder if both of us were wrong about ourselves," she tried a different angle. "You say you live for my sake only, but are we such weak individuals? For my own part, I must live my life intensely, and you are hardly a timid, apathetic person. Otherwise you would never have survived all the hard work that has brought you success. You are strong by nature, a person who sticks to his convictions. The problem is that you try too hard, and against your nature, to do things for my sake. We should be and act according to our own nature, and then we would feel much more comfortable, and our relationship would become more honest. What you ought to do is to insist on your right to live your own life fully."

"You can think whatever you want. You've seen the truth about me, and you know my mind has been settled since we married. When the time comes, I need only to act on my resolution." Tsukuda's response was always the same.

By 'resolution' he implied either killing himself or giving everything up and returning to his native rural town. Since Nobuko couldn't tell how serious he was, she had no choice but to stop pursuing it. She worried that he might be in earnest and wondered if this psychological battle would last till one of them died. But other times she decided he was merely bluffing, and then she would curtsey and smile and say, "I see. Well then, please go ahead."

It was already July. Tsukuda was to leave on a short business trip. He had almost nothing he needed for the trip, and because their relationship was in such an unsettled state, Nobuko wanted him to go in reasonable style. She took all the money she had and went shopping with Tamotsu, who happened to be visiting her that day.

The day was hot but there was a nice breeze. A Mitsukoshi Department Store flag was flapping cheerfully in the blue sky. Nobuko finished her shopping in an hour.

"What do you want to do now? Go back home?" she asked her brother.

"It doesn't matter to me," Tamotsu said.

"It'll be late if we return to Akasaka now. How about walking a bit on Ginza?"

Tamotsu agreed, looking very pleased.

They went to Shiseidō and had an ice cream soda. Nobuko handed two straws to Tamotsu and took another two for herself.

"Try this new way of drinking with straws. You blow with one to make bubbles and drink with the other," she said.

"Oh?" He put the two straws into his mouth. Then dropped them right away. "Wait a minute, this isn't right. I don't know how. Can you do it and show me?"

"It's easy. Like this, see?" Nobuko blew until the bubbles started overflowing.

"Really?" Tamotsu looked into his sister's glass with a serious face. When he realized that the soda water did not go up in the second straw until the first one was blowing the bubbles, he started laughing. "I thought so. I knew you couldn't exhale and inhale at the same time," he said, pleased with himself. Nobuko laughed, too.

"You realized it right away, didn't you? I kept trying for a long time," she said.

"When was that?"

"A long time ago. I was tricked by an old man, a Westerner."

After putting Tamotsu on the streetcar heading to Ueno, Nobuko caught hers to head home. It was still early in the afternoon and there were not many passengers in the car. She watched the scenery along the moat from the wide open window. The sky was a summery light blue, transparent. The texture and the color of the heavy stone walls, the smooth lawns, and the dense, dark green of old pine trees, were all reflected in the water of the gently curving moat. They created the harmonious beauty of traditional Japan and Nobuko felt tranquil and subdued, a touch of gaiety surfacing in her from time to time.

There was a woman sitting opposite Nobuko. Her dark-colored clothes of good quality, her soft hair, and even her *geta* clogs showed good taste and modesty. Nobuko judged her to be thirty-seven or eight. Her umbrella was also dark. The woman's meticulous appearance and a certain warmth shone through her modest attire. Making herself comfortable in her seat, she also looked out the window at the scenery. When she noticed that Nobuko was watching her, she returned the look openly and naturally. Their eyes met. The way she regarded Nobuko was serene and warm; her light-brown eyes were pleasant.

As she continued to look at the woman, Nobuko began noticing strange feelings surging up inside of her. She felt the woman's calm and generous spirit spreading toward her. She thought that the pain she had been experiencing would be understood at once if she uttered even a single word to this woman, if she said, "Look, I. . . ."—the distressing state she was in would miraculously be resolved.

Nobuko didn't look away, and the woman kept her light-brown eyes on her, steady and serene. As the woman's glances fell upon her forehead and cheeks, Nobuko had the sensation of being caressed. She wanted to get up and go to her. As she struggled with herself, her heart started pounding. She knew she wouldn't go to the woman, and yet she could not turn her eyes away. Once she had read a Russian novel in which a man suddenly started telling his story to a total stranger in the compartment of the train. At the time, Nobuko was skeptical that such a scene could actually take place. Now she understood how the man felt: full of anguish like I am now, she thought.

Nobuko was relieved when the streetcar came to her stop. Stepping from the car onto the street, she could not calm herself. She looked up at the window as if she were turning back to find something unexpected. She couldn't see the woman; her view was blocked by the khaki uniform of a soldier.

"Would you write me a letter . . . to Dōsaka?"

"Well, I don't know if I'll have time. . . . You'd find my letters uninteresting, anyway," Tsukuda replied.

Two days later he went on his trip. Nobuko went to Dōzaka.

Original title: *Nobuko* (1925).

Hirabayashi Taiko

(1905–1971)

IN SEPTEMBER 1923, when the Great Kantō Earthquake shook Tokyo, killing one hundred thousand people, Hirabayashi Taiko had been living in the city a little over a year. She was eighteen years old. For a few days after the earthquake, while most sensible people were leaving Tokyo to find safer places, Taiko and her common-law husband, an ex-Christian and unemployed anarchist, roamed the city to see the aftermath of the destruction. Along with horrifying glimpses of grotesquely burned bodies, there were other scenes, such as the burned police headquarters and the partially destroyed mint, which in her view exhibited poetic justice. This independent spirit and irrepressible curiosity of the young Hirabayashi Taiko would also characterize the writer who was to emerge several years later.

Taiko grew up in a small village in the mountainous region of central Japan. She was a bright child and a good pupil with an unquenchable thirst for reading. She devoured any book she could lay her hands on: Dostoevsky, Chekov, Tolstoy, Hamsun, Zola, and Maupassant. She had the privilege of studying under a young and enthusiastic teacher, who pointed out to Taiko, his best student, that there were other options she could choose after primary school besides working in the silk-reeling factory, like most of the girls of her village, or getting married, like her two older sisters. He also taught her another crucial lesson: freedom through writing.

Both Taiko's father, who spent most of his life dealing with the business failures of his own father, and her mother, an uneducated and subservient woman, discouraged Taiko from pursuing her education. In spite of their opposition, she took the high school entrance exam and was enrolled. This was

Taiko's first deliberate step toward the fiercely uncompromising life she was to lead. Her desire to learn and to shape her own future was coupled with an idealistic nature, and she found herself drawn to leftist ideology while in high school. She read Marx's *Das Kapital* and joined a local group of leftist revolutionaries; she also subscribed to a literary journal produced by the most radical activists in Tokyo and contributed fiction to a coterie journal. Thoroughly convinced that the existing social system was inherently evil, Taiko decided to go to Tokyo to make direct contacts with activists in the central arena. Going to Tokyo was in fact the only option open to Taiko; the other path to an independent life—becoming a teacher, a common approach for aspiring young women—was closed to her because of her association with leftist groups.

Taiko eventually found a job in Tokyo as a telephone operator. Her salary was meager, barely enough to pay room and board, but she had taken the job because of an advertisement offering English lessons for employees, which proved to be false. Within three months she lost this job after being caught talking on the phone with Sakai Toshihiko, a renowned socialist. Another socialist friend helped her find a better job as a bookstore clerk, but before long she was forced to give up the position on account of the unpopular behavior of her lover. The lover was the first man Taiko became sexually involved with, and that may have been the reason she found it difficult to leave him; it may also have been because she felt sorry for someone who was shunned by others. Motivated more by compassion than by love, Taiko moved from one city to another with this lover, always looking for jobs. Eventually they went as far as Manchuria, then occupied by the Japanese military.

In 1924, Taiko returned from Manchuria alone, after having given birth to the only child she would ever have and losing him less than a month later in a charity hospital. She left behind her lover, who had been imprisoned for writing a document containing dangerous criticism of the Emperor. The Manchurian experience left Taiko with a sense of guilt that would haunt her for a long time.

She came back to Tokyo with a renewed resolution to write, but three years were to pass before she felt sufficiently confident to begin in earnest. In the meantime she became entangled in several difficult relationships with men who were as irresponsible and parasitic as her first lover. With her time and energy spent on supporting herself as well as the current lover, she found little time to write. After trying many different jobs, she settled on waitressing at cafés. At that time, the café was a new type of establishment in Japan, a combination coffee house, restaurant and bar. It was considered unfit for decent women to work in cafés, but the pay was adequate and for Taiko it meant a chance to write in her spare time. Still, her situation was anything but stable, and she had to move from one café to another when former lovers came and tried to extort money from her, beating her if she was unable or unwilling to cooperate.

Through her lover, Taiko associated with a group of anarchists as well as leftist activists. Some of them believed that capitalists owed them a living, since their profits were the result of exploitation. Basing their views on theories they had read in Kropotkin's *Spoliation of Bread*, they managed to extort small amounts of money from businesses and banks. Rejecting all bourgeois conventions, including sexual morality, they led decadent, hand-to-mouth lives. When hungry, they would steal food, taking vegetables from someone's garden, for example. They borrowed money whenever they could, with no intention of repaying it. They would gather at certain cafés, ordering water and drinking it with the sugar provided on the table until someone with money came and bought them something better. Among the poor poets, anarchists and writers whom Taiko met during those soirees was Hayashi Fumiko, who became her lifetime friend and rival. Fumiko, who would become a very successful writer, taught Taiko how to sell stories to the editors of various magazines.

Taiko and Fumiko discovered that they shared much the same fate: they were beleaguered by poverty and exploitative lovers and possessed by a desire to write. For a brief period, when they managed to rid themselves of their lovers, they rented a room together. They even shared one outfit of clothing, each wearing it in turn when going out to see editors. When they could not sell their stories, they would walk the many miles back home, unable to afford streetcar fare.

Unlike Fumiko, who was able to write while she was involved in chaotic love affairs, Taiko became so drained from her emotional upheavals with men that her creative activities were hampered. At the end of 1927, Taiko resolved to put an end to her life of unstable relationships and asked her married friends to be matchmakers for her. The result was her marriage to a socialist named Kobori Jinji. Kobori, a simple, self-educated man with a working-class background, was more responsible than Taiko's previous lovers, but he did not have a steady job and was more often than not dependent on her income from writing. Taiko struggled to learn to love this man, only to be bitterly disappointed many years later when she was confronted by the child he had fathered with their former maid.

While working as a waitress, Taiko wrote detective stories and juvenile fiction, which she was able to sell readily. Her talent as a story teller was evident and a few editors encouraged her to write more of this popular fiction in order to establish her place in the genre. Taiko felt, however, that her real calling was serious literature. The wide range of her experiences, most of which would have been simply unthinkable for women of previous generations, gave her a unique chance to study the people around her and was a source of inspiration for her more developed writing. In 1927 Taiko won first prize in the New Writer's Award contest for her story, "Self-Mockery" (*Azakeru*), and this was a major breakthrough—she received 200 yen in prize money, enough for a couple to live on for several months. A largely autobiographical story, "Self-Mockery" conveys a strange mixture of despair and nonchalant bravado, a sense of rebellion both idealistic and cynical. The young woman protagonist wants to believe that the poor are incorruptible and that she will never surrender to the social mores which have kept women unenlightened. She despises middle-class values and is contemptuous of social conventions, yet she recognizes her own muddled life is equally a target of mockery.

"In the Charity Ward" (Seryōshitsu nite), another prize-winning piece written in 1927, is based on Taiko's Manchurian experience. The protagonist, a self-proclaimed socialist, has been arrested as an accomplice to a political crime, but she is placed in a hospital rather than a prison because she is about to deliver her baby. Because she is a charity patient, however, the hospital authorities refuse to supply her with cow's milk, even though she is afflicted with beriberi. Her baby dies while she is breast-feeding him. The story is an attack on bureaucratic rigidity and the inhumane treatment of the poor at an institution run by Christians. It was published in the left-wing literary journal Literary Front (Bungei Sensen) and established her reputation as a proletarian writer.

Taiko also wrote stories about women factory workers on strike and about the peasants' struggles against landowners. "Diary of Members of the Opposition Faction" (Hi-kambu-ha no Nikki, 1927) tells about a couple of poor, uneducated socialists, who cannot go along with the formal teachings of a Marxist group. They are skeptical of what they hear at study sessions and what they see in prison; they distrust the leaders who seem to be satisfied with merely the rhetoric of class struggle. Taiko shared this skepticism, which she particularly felt toward the more radical faction of the leftist leaders, which included several writers. The proletarian school of writing advocated the theory that political ideology had to override personal sentiments. Taiko could not swallow this dogma and twice left the leftist writers group over disagreements on views of literature. Keenly interested in the complexity of human nature as well as in the relationship between the individual and society, Taiko put these interests above ideological concerns. "The Railroad Workers" (Shisetsu Ressha, 1929), for example, is more than a story about Chinese railroad workers and their successful work sabotage; it is also about the mystery of the human mind as manifested in the workers, who are tyrannized by a mechanism that they cannot understand. The story's central image of the vast, untamed Manchurian plain creates a vividly eerie atmosphere. In a story entitled "Sorrowful Love" (*Kanashiki Aijō*, 1931), Taiko examined the dilemmas of love and class struggle, presenting the difficult conflicts between human emotion and political ideology. Taiko's own sympathies in this story are clearly on the side of love.

For ten long years, beginning when she was thirty-two, Taiko endured continual illnesses and police interrogations because of her political beliefs. For all conscientious writers refusing to cooperate with the military state, these were years of silence. In 1946 her voice was restored with the publication of "This Kind of Woman" (*Kōiu Onna*), a story for which she was honored with the prestigious Women's Literary Award. In this work, which stood out amidst the devastated post-World War II literary scene, Taiko succeeds in creating a fully developed character whose strength is measured in terms of her self-awareness and her ability to share herself with her loved ones. The year the story was published, Taiko adopted her husband's niece. From this year until her death from breast cancer at the age of sixty-three, Taiko was extremely productive. She expanded her repertoire to include non-political writings that reached a wide audience and she established herself as an important and well-known literary and social critic. Even though she became quite a respected figure in her later years, Taiko always maintained friendships with people of different backgrounds and classes; she was well-liked by intellectuals as well as workers, and even had a friend from the *yazuka*, the Japanese underworld. Her interest in social and political issues remained strong, and in 1955, the same year she divorced Kobori, she became involved in the movement to abolish legal prostitution. Her autobiographical novel, *A Flower in the Desert* (*Sabaku no Hana*), was published in 1957 and here Taiko reveals her life in its full range—her early struggles for independence and her series of destructive relationships with men, the pain and joy of creative and political activity, and, most impressively, her endurance and unfailing trust in herself as a woman and an artist.

Throughout her life, the central topic in Taiko's fiction was the condition of women, and her stories are filled with strong and determined women characters. Taiko's fierce and uncompromising independence, her vitality and resilient spirit set her apart from the women writers of the previous generation and from many of her contemporaries. As much as any writer of the 1920s and 1930s, she represented the radical spirit that became an important voice in modern Japanese literature.

Y. T.

Self-Mockery

translated by Yukiko Tanaka

With a hand on my shabby winter kimono pressing against my left breast, I walk with faltering steps. I have been walking like this for some time, resisting the temptation to open the front of the kimono to see what might be causing the pain. It seems to be coming from somewhere deep inside the breast. The street stretching in front of me is covered by a thin mask of dust: it has the look of a second-hand furniture store. When I get to the corner bakery where a khaki awning hangs all the way down to prevent the dust from coming in, I stop and look at my breast, unable to resist the temptation any longer. Like a balloon that's lost its air, it hangs there loosely. Just as an old scar tells of pain once endured, my breast shows that it has once nursed. I hate looking at these breasts, for I see there, on the sagging skin, the clear image of my ugly self. But I don't find anything wrong with my left breast now. As I close the front of the kimono and resume walking, I again feel the surge of self-disgust whirling up inside of me.

Perhaps I've been walking with a faint sneer on my face, exposing my yellow teeth. People turn around as they pass, to take another look at me, a strange-looking woman. "Who could stop a boulder rolling down from the top of a mountain?" I utter these words which come to my mind out of nowhere. Repeating the words over and over, I walk aimlessly. My eyes fix on the faces of the passersby with the rudeness of a fly that stays on your skin. This keeps the scenes of the last night and this morning from coming back to my mind like a ball of yarn spitting out an endless thread.

A brown streetcar covered by a layer of dust approaches, ringing a loud bell to warn the man who is digging up the ground between the rails. The man swings his pickax up and down mechanically as if he were a doll on a spring; he does not hear the bell and the expression on his sweaty face, languid as a high noon of late spring days, does not change.

"Watch out, you fool," shouts the conductor, showing his irritation as he winds the emergency brake. The streetcar has momentum and does not stop right away; the old conductor becomes desperate. When I come out of my reverie, I am staring at the streetcar which has stopped in the middle of the street right in front of the construction worker. They are within touching distance from each other.

"A brake that cannot stop the car," I say to myself. Both this expression and the one about the boulder that cannot be halted are apt descriptions of my present circumstances. Then, remembering the desperate look on the face of the conductor, I smile and say to myself, "My own brake cannot stop anything, even if I try harder than that old conductor." I want to burst out laughing.

Ever since I left Yada's apartment I've been walking, not knowing exactly where I was heading, but now it looks like I'm near Dōgenzaka. Divided by the stream of cars, pedestrians are walking down both sides of the street, loathsome expressions on their faces, moving their sweaty bodies and kicking the skirts of their full-length winter kimonos.

In my eyes this busy street filled with greasy faces of hot, excited people is a vivid pattern of many colors. I feel I am the only one who doesn't harmonize. I am a solid, grey thread.

The face powder that stains the collar of my kimono bothers me. Not having had enough sleep the previous night, I am exhausted. Although I have a one yen bill in my pocket—the money Yada gave me—I don't feel like spending it on train fare. But at the top of the hill I can no longer walk and so I wait at a streetcar stop.

Inside, the streetcar is stuffy, filled with the odor of sweating young men. Hanging onto a strap, I call forth Yada—his face and his scant hair—and I draw his image on the steamy windowpane. I find, surprisingly, that the evocation of his face is no longer so disturbing. It could just as well have been a picture of a total stranger drawn on a piece of paper by someone else.

"Is this my true self: an ugly woman?" I ask myself calmly.

The streetcar jerks, throwing me toward the young man holding the strap next to me. The movement is so sudden that most of the standing passengers lose their balance. The young man, too, falls sharply against the man standing on his other side. The way I totter, however, is ridiculous. The young man is wearing a fine spring suit and he carries a walking stick on his left arm. He gives me a quick glance and then straightens his head and concentrates on the advertisement in front of his eyes. He might be sneering, I think as I look up at the side of his face. I have often seen young men sneer the minute they passed by me, disappointed at what they have just seen. This young man seems to be the kind who classifies women by their appearance, who enjoys golf and going to parties at the Imperial Hotel.

When the streetcar stops at the next station, I lean over him, and when it starts up, I press my face against his arm, feeling the soft fabric of his suit. When he finally realizes that the shabby-looking woman next to him is leaning against him deliberately, the young man frowns, stares at me for a second, then moves to the next strap. I move down one strap too, pretending it is a natural course of action. Shocked, the young man looks around as if seeking witnesses to my peculiar act. When the passenger who was sitting in front of him gets off, the young man takes the empty seat in an ungentleman-like way, pushing me away with his elbow. So, when the streetcar makes another jerky movement, I place my hand right on his thigh, pretending that I simply couldn't help it. The young man, hate clearly showing on his pale face, looks at me for a moment, stands up and walks to the door. I take his seat, feeling pleased, as if something refreshing flowed down into my chest.

The conductor comes around to sell tickets; I give him the crumpled one yen bill Yada gave me, muttering to myself, "I wonder if you know how this bill came to me." I feel strange somehow, and stare at the conductor.

"One yen bill, eh? I'm not sure I have change," he says, holding the bill in one hand and opening his purse with the other.

"Where are you going?"

"To . . ."

"And where did you get on, Miss?"

"At Ōhashi." I respond smoothly.

"Ōhashi?" he says, giving me a quick glance. Then he starts counting coins onto my palm. I lose my composure and feel the blood surging up to my head. Seeing that I'm upset, the conductor seems to have decided that I lied about where I got on. He gives me another sharp look before he moves on. I did not lose my composure because I had told him a lie. When he gave me that sparkling look typical of young men, I hesitated, sensing that he had seen everything I had pushed away to the back of my mind. The conductor wore a silver-colored medal around his neck and his long hair showed under his hat. The contour of his face, with his well-shaped nose, was pleasing. All in all he was quite good-looking. I feel relieved after he leaves; I am able to fold my arms and relax.

"But that was a legitimate one yen bill, properly issued by the Bank of Japan," I tell the conductor silently as I get off the streetcar. Instead of verbalizing it, I smile at him.

After I get off the streetcar, I walk away from the main street and come to a fish store. Inside the dark store I stand for a long time, staring at the fish displayed with their glittering scales. The proprietor of the store stands patiently, waiting for me to say something. But I don't say a word, feeling sick at the sight of the red salmon filets that have two yellow flies on them. The man looks at me doubtfully and starts walking toward the back of the store.

"Oh, I want this one, please," I say abruptly. The man waves a few sticks of burning incense over the fish to get rid of the flies. Some dried-out fish scales stick to his hand. I leave the fish store, and as I'm walking along, I think about my strange conduct in the streetcar. I cannot help smiling.

It's late afternoon when I return, my face grey with dust, to the barber shop behind a bamboo field, where I rent a room on the second floor. My mind is stretched out, vacant. I tell myself, "Something will work out. I just have to go on doing what I can." I cannot find any other words of consolation for myself. I go inside without making any noise and take off my *geta* clogs. Koyama sees me when he comes down to use the bathroom.

"Where have you been? Wandering around all this time?" he says, not realizing that the old landlady is working in the next room. His voice is surprisingly loud. I do not respond, but the old woman lifts her inflamed eyes from her sewing and looks at me, a woman who did not come home the night before.

"I was out there doing things you can't imagine, simply to keep us together; I did it because I want to be with you." Composing sentences like these in my mind, I go up the stairs, silent. Since morning I have repeated these words to myself, the words with which someone who understands my actions might console me. I have even secretly enjoyed the sense of beauty that accompanies this dark despair of mine. Now my legs are heavy as if they were chained.

The women who casts her chastity away in order to save her marriage has been approved throughout our history. Her sacrifice has even been praised as a sign of womanly virtue. In my case, however, it is different. I do not have a claim upon Koyama that warrants such sacrifice. Besides, I am a woman who has known three men, each of whom I left without much agony. Koyama, who abandoned a communist group after two imprisonments, has been writing and producing large numbers of unsolicited manuscripts over the past four years. He sends them off tirelessly; they are, however, all returned one after another as if there were rubber bands attached to them. He is a wretched man who conceals his real reason for living with me, namely to live off my earnings.

"Can't you go to someone you know and ask for just a little? I won't ask again," he pleads every time we find ourselves with no money. He looks at me, narrowing his attractive eyes in an attempt to read my mind. Each time he promises "not again" or "only this time," but there have been too many "the last time's."

"I can't do that," I tell him curtly and look straight into his face, scornfully. By "someone" he means the men I had sexual relationships with in the past. Yesterday, too, we exchanged the same words till I got impatient and decided to do exactly what he asked me to. I had already told him that Yada had refused to loan me money. No sense giving money to a woman who lives another man, Yada said.

Still wearing my dirty socks, I sit on the tatami floor which is old and discolored, a pale yellow. From the window I see the strong afternoon sun through the bamboos, casting lines on the wet soil. I listen for the footsteps of Koyama coming up the stairs but there is no sound. Perhaps he has gone somewhere. While I sit and gaze outside the window, I become aware of how thirsty I am. Many thoughts go through my mind.

I wanted to believe the axiom which states that "the just are poor." I once knew a working-class woman who had no understanding of her husband's position; everytime he joined a strike, she railed against him. "Only fools are agitated into destructive action," she would say, scornfully. Though the husband was not the type to be easily affected by his wife's words, there were times when I saw he was deeply disturbed. The invisible pressure that such women exert upon their husbands must help the workers lose many a battle against the capitalists. Those women cannot help themselves—the pressure of the old customs, internalized, encourages their conservative views—but I found it difficult to suppress my disgust whenever I encountered one of them. I had wondered on occasion if I shared their attitudes. But in the case of my relationship with Koyama, the situation was reversed. In fact I nearly called him a waif once in order to humiliate him. Although my past was not without stains, that should not allow Koyama to get the upper hand in our relationship. He puts the burden of bringing in money on my shoulders because he looks down on me. To him I am a woman who has so many blemishes that she has no choice but to please her man in whatever way she can.

And as for me, I have worn myself out trying to find a man who lived up to my idealistic notions. In the process I have lost a fresh attitude toward my own life. I feel wretched; I am a woman who has lost self-control, who is persuaded by the trifling force of a hair. I had a child by the man who was my first love. The child, born on a rusty bed in a dismal charity hospital room in Manchuria, died, like a candle blown out, while I was bedridden with post-delivery beriberi. The child's father had been taken to prison, accused for something he himself had not quite understood. That happened on the morning of my first labor pains. My life of restless wandering began then.

The sagging skin of my abdomen is evidence that I delivered a child. My breasts are as limp as the dead body of a cat. At the bottom of my suitcase is a small box containing an urn wrapped in a piece of imitation brocade. I, a woman who left her first lover in a cold prison cell and then went from one man to another as if guided by some unknown force, have not been able to discard this small box which, when I shake it, makes a faint rattling sound as a toy would. More than a few times Koyama and I have exchanged foul words over this little box. He has accepted my past in his rational mind, but his weak nature dictates that he return to that time in my life whenever he needs to defend his position in our relationship.

Sitting alone and reminiscing about my past causes tears to well up in my eyes. What was it that made me do what I did, I ask once again, but there is no strength left in me to think it through. I find myself adrift in an ocean of fatigue, I feel engulfed by a wasteland. Again, I feel a sharp pain like a gimlet boring deep inside my left breast. Ever since that morning, everything around me has been fuzzy, without contour. Only this pain touches my sensitized nerves like a needle. The fresh yellow luster of the bamboos reflects the hazy, late afternoon sun and moves gently with the slightest breeze. I yearn for a

glass of water and yet lack the will to get up and go downstairs.

"Did you stay at Yada's apartment?" are the first words
Koyama utters, coldly, as he enters the room.

"I was going to leave but I wanted to get money for the
streetcar. He said he had no money but a friend of his was
supposed to come in the morning."

"You knew I didn't have money even for a pack of cigarettes."

"Yes, I knew. That's why I wanted to borrow even a few
yen . . ." I say, and I hold my breast as if I cannot tolerate the
pain.

"What's the matter?"

"My breast hurts."

"Did it happen just now?"

"No. Since this morning." As soon as I say this, I realize I've
made a mistake.

"Because you stayed at Yada's, I bet," he says spitefully, and
averts his face.

"What did you say?" I turn to face him directly and say
calmly. "I went to Yada's because you told me to."

"And did you get money?" He stares at my face for a moment as if trying to discover what might have happened the
night before. The next moment, however, I see by his expression that he's decided nothing happened.

"No, I didn't."

"Nothing?" he sounds as if money is a matter of life and
death.

"Only the streetcar fare." I answer, thinking of the fifty sen
in my pocket. Somehow I cannot tell him that Yada gave me
one yen; I feel ashamed. When I left my apartment in the
morning, I was resolved to let Yada have whatever he wanted
of me. It was an order; I had to help my man even if it meant
sacrificing myself, I thought; I even felt heroic. In my resolution, however, was also a secret desire for revenge, a desire to
control the man who was so spineless. And practically speak-
ing, there was no other way for us to get money.

But as it turned out, I responded differently. I felt ludicrous—here I was trying so hard to get so little money, and for a man like Koyama. It was debasing. With this realization I was able to see things with a new perspective. Up to that point I had harbored a ray of hope about my life with Koyama. But revitalized with the naive optimism of my youth, I decided not to ask Yada for money. That night in his room, I listened to Yada's breathing and was reminded of an animal. I was awake throughout the night, thinking of the new life I would start by myself and rehearsing the strong words I would throw at Koyama when I announced my resolution.

By the time I left Yada's apartment the following morning, however, my resolution was shattered, proof that it was mere illusion. As I was preparing to leave, Yada seemed to remember his promise and grudgingly took one yen out of his wallet and stuck it out in front of me. I thought he said something like, "Well, then," but it was not clear. Undefinable words of self-mockery, droning like cicadas, slowly filled my body and I came back to Koyama in a daze.

Using a pair of tongs to poke around the ash in the charcoal brazier, Koyama finds a stained cigarette butt which is still long enough to smoke.

"Why don't you go and buy some." Yawning I tell him as I take the fifty sen coin from my pocket.

"Is this all you got from him?" Koyama stares at the coin as if it were a rare kind. Then he goes out to buy cigarettes, making a squeaking sound on the stairs.

I open the window to let some air into the stuffy room. Light from the lamp repeats the square shape of the window on the dark ground. Young bamboo shoots covered with brown husks grow here and there. I haven't seen them for a few days and the young, thick shoots that remind me of the strong arms of young men have grown considerably. I hear mosquitos humming, invigorated by the warm, humid weather. Attracted by the human smell, and the light, they now come flying into the room. Suddenly I remember the days, also at this time of the year, when I was lying in a room of the Women's Home in Manchuria. I felt restless under the discolored and stained old mosquito net, not knowing what to do with myself as my body recovered from the delivery. That was two years ago, and the wanderlust that entered my blood then is still with me, unabated.

"Why don't we have bamboo shoots cooked in rice tonight?" I say to Koyama when he comes back with a cigarette in his mouth.

"But a small bamboo shoot would cost at least twenty sen," he says light-heartedly. His mood seems to have changed.

"Really? Are they that expensive?" I respond in a tone equally carefree, smiling. The bamboo shoots that I saw at the green-grocers looked delicious; they appealed to my appetite, which had not been good lately.

"We are at the end of our rope if we have to argue over twenty sen," I say and look up at him, cajolingly. I feel a certain warmth toward this man who is so easily deceived, who loses whatever discerning power he has with the smallest effort at pretense on my part.

"We have salted fish."

"We can't be eating salted fish every day."

"You are extravagant." He smiles, showing his good mood. I smile, too, but coaxingly. Smiling, I feel the memory of last night retiring to the back of my mind as if a crumpled paper were being pushed away. "That was nothing," says a voice inside me. "The real vice is something else, nothing like that." I have experienced many men and their memories are marked on my flesh. That is why I have become insensate. I can't feel pain other than in an intellectualized way.

After we finished a dinner of two pieces of oily fish, we go downstairs, trying not to make any noise. We are going to the bamboo field to steal bamboo shoots which we have seen from our window. A young barber is playing the violin on the windowsill of the room facing the field. This man had a lover who worked at a café and though he was quite serious about her, his parents would not consent to the marriage. Whenever Koyama and I go out together, he watches us enviously. His violin under his chin, he looks up and stares at us; the gleam I recognize in his eyes seems particularly vivid tonight, perhaps because the warm season is starting.

"We mustn't be seen," Koyama says, meaning the young barber.

"We can't enter from the other side of the field, then." We walk along the hedge where pale white quince flowers are blooming here and there.

"Let's go in here," I say and stoop with both of my hands on the ground, trying to squeeze through a hole in the hedge.

"Don't drop the scarf," Koyama's voice is behind me. While I'm searching for suitable shoots, he breaks a big one, making a distinctive noise. In the stagnating air that is filled with a fragrance coming either from sprouting vegetation or the moist ground, it sounds like a popped balloon. Alarmed by the noise he's made, Koyama runs into the hedge. On the other side of the hedge a dog has started barking. Koyama loses his composure; he wiggles his torso to get out of the hole and gets stuck. The dog lowers his head and barks louder. I whistle and look over the hedge, and there I see a fierce black-and-white dog pacing back and forth. Koyama runs and the dog is on his heels.

I leave the bamboo field through the hole in the hedge, three bamboo shoots wrapped in my scarf. When the initial comic surprise has passed, I get angry at Koyama's behavior. Through the barber's window I see the upper body of the old woman who is standing in the middle of the room and shining a lamp toward me.

"It's humid, isn't it?" I remark as I walk past the window.

"Yes, it is," the old woman responds. Her bleary eyes peer into the distance, where a dog's barking is faintly heard.

"It's spooky to hear a dog barking at night," she is saying to her son, at the bottom of the stairs. On my way up to my room I hear the son, who is whetting razors, answer his mother half-heartedly.

It is more than half an hour later when Koyama returns with his kimono torn at the sleeves. His knees are dirty and his hands are bleeding where he was scratched by thorns.

"It was awful," he says frowning, and tries to shake the dirt from his kimono.

"The dog wouldn't bark like that if you didn't get so flustered," I say, pushing back with my knees the papers that I had shoved underneath the desk. I had started writing a letter to Yada, assuming that Koyama had gone to see one of his friends.

"I did what you wanted, didn't I? So you ought to lend me fifteen yen as you promised. I'm sure you'd agree that a poor woman in this society has no choice but to throw away her only possession in order to survive. If you are a man with the conscience of a true revolutionary, you must admit that is true. Please loan me fifteen yen. You are one of the bourgeoisie, after all; you have parents who send you a hundred yen a month. You're a carefree man who is satisfied to discuss theories," I have said in the letter. I wonder if Yada will be angry but decide to go ahead and write more. When Koyama comes back, I hide the letter underneath the desk among other papers.

"It's the end of the month tomorrow," Koyama says, peeling a blue page from the daily calender.

"We've got to pay some rent tomorrow, Yoshiko. Otherwise, they'll kick us out."

"I guess," I reply, absent-mindedly. We haven't paid the rent for three months, not even the fifteen yen we have promised at the beginning of the first month.

"I wonder if Yada has any money."

"He probably does." Koyama looks annoyed at my brusque reply but doesn't say anything. A cat meows on the tin roof; its cry is an agony of intense yearnings.

"Shall we go to bed?" Koyama asks.

"Yes, let's go to bed." As I lift my face casually, my eyes meet his, and they are filled with tears that come from yawning. The next moment he looks down, embarrassed. There is that peculiar radiance in his eyes, passion, which had penetrated me when I was living with a painter of the Expressionist School. In those fleeting days when he courted me, Koyama used to send me secret glances when the painter was not paying attention to us.

While Koyama, wearing a woman's kimono as pajamas, is pulling the curtain, I spread our bedding. The old crumpled sheet in front of me brings to mind a vivid picture of myself in Yada's room at around this time last night. Pulling the damp quilt cover over my head I feel enveloped in a sordid passion. "I wish I would meet a man I could throw my whole self into," I think as I draw pictures of men one after another. "Say, Yoshiko. Honey," I imagine someone calling in the distance. It's the voice of the man I left in Manchuria. "This way, come this way," I plead and pull myself closer to the mirage of the ideal lover I have created.

"Yoshiko, we're having bamboo shoots for breakfast, aren't we?" Koyama asks, trying to catch a chance for conversation.

"Yes. We haven't had bamboo shoots for some time. So it should be a treat," I answer gently, in an attempt to be affectionate. "Meoooow," the cat cries and walks across the roof directly above us. Koyama gets up and turns off the light.

The shade from the bamboo, which earlier had gently waved across the entire curtain, slowly recedes to the lower part as the sun rises. A sunbeam shimmers through the crack of the curtain, casting long lines across the tatami floor. I have awakened to the sound of dried fish being shaved. "What goal should I have today to make me get through the day? What could I look forward to?" These questions pass through my mind. In the low alcove where there is no proper hanging scroll nor ornament I see some coins shining dully in the morning light.

"Forty-four sen." I count them. The change Koyama brought back after buying his cigarettes.

"Mr. Koyama, there's a letter for you, a registered letter. Can you come down?" the barber calls.

"Yes." Awakened by the call, Koyama answers in a screechy voice, and then says to me, "Hey, it's a registered letter."

"You go, please. I can't go like this. Besides my hair is a mess."

"Please hurry." The young barber's voice sounds fretful. I sense in his high-pitched voice a certain irrational protest toward us, a young couple who stay in bed till late in the morning. Koyama gets up reluctantly and goes downstairs in his woman's cotton kimono with one torn sleeve.

"Rejected manuscript again," he says when he comes back, and throws the thick brown envelope and a printed card on the floor.

"I told you it's a waste of postage."

"Why don't you get up? It's very late."

"I will."

"Get up." He is standing right next to me.

"I said I will. Don't shout like that. It's too early."

"Disgusting. You're a slut, you know."

Getting out of bed, I go downstairs to wash my face. Standing by the well, I spit some tooth paste onto the concrete slab: it is pink with blood from a sore on my gum. As I look up at the sun to guess the time, I hear the clock strike eleven. Back in the room I chop the bamboo shoot while Koyama shaves dried fish to make a stock, holding the plane on his knee. He is wearing his winter kimono which is dirty with grease spots. Both of us are perspiring a little. I think about my light wool kimono, which I could wear now that it's warmer were it not being held hostage in a pawn shop for three yen. The smoothness and fresh smell of the light weight wool makes me think of young men's body odor. My attachment to that kimono is more urgent now than to any human being I have known.

Just as we finish our breakfast we hear the old man calling Koyama from downstairs.

"He's calling you."

"It must be about the rent." Looking at me nervously Koyama stands up, and with a pack of cigarettes in his hand reluctantly goes downstairs.

"Are you busy, Mr. Koyama?" I hear the vibrant voice of the old man, a retired mason.

"Oh, hello," Koyama answers sheepishly.

"According to the today's paper, General Tanaka has finally decided to go into politics." The old man is talkative. I stop listening to the conversation and tear up the letter to Yada, which I have pulled out from underneath the desk. I examine the torn pieces and tear them even smaller. No sense writing a letter because he wouldn't lend me money anyway. I want to laugh at myself for having been so deluded as to write that letter. "Somehow I thought I was special, and that's why I was deceived by those men," I say to myself, thinking about my past. "What good would it do to tell a man like Yada, who's as shameless as a stray cat, that he is a bourgeois. Any bourgeois, whom Yada claims are his enemies, wouldn't begrudge five or ten yen when it comes to buying a woman. And yet, he. . . ." Thinking about Yada and then about my own situation makes me feel disgusted with myself. I take my kimono out of the closet and quickly put it on while Koyama is still downstairs. Just like yesterday, the kimono is wrinkled, and the collar is stained with face powder.

"Newspaper? Could you wait for a few more days?" I shout down from the window to the paper boy who is outside saying something to me. Standing in the middle of the road by the bamboo field and looking up, he looks like he is pleading with me to pardon him. He has received no payment from us for the past two months. "Of course I'll pay when I have money. Don't be a pest, all right?" I shout, smiling, and then close the window. I feel awful afterwards. "Well, I've got to get fifteen yen or so from Yada," I say to myself, remembering the expression on Yada's face. I feel a surge of anger, and grit my teeth.

"That old man isn't so bad," Koyama says, coming back upstairs. He seems to be feeling better.

"Why do you say that?"

"He said he would wait for the rent till the fifteenth. 'If there isn't any money, what can you do?' he said."

That's nothing to feel good about, I think to myself, and leave the room without saying anything to Koyama, who had not expected me to go out so early.

The street looks just as unclean and dusty as it did the day

before, and the streetcar is filled with the oppressive odor of
male bodies. "I wonder if I can spot another one of those
gentlemen who is offended by my shabbiness and ugliness?" I
say to myself while I wait for the streetcar, remembering the
comic scene of the previous day. The people waiting for the
streetcar squint to protect their eyes from the glaring sun and
dust, and when the streetcar comes, they get on, pushing other
passengers as if they were fighting for their lives. Men shove
women out of their way so that they can hang on to the car;
they look like locusts. In front of a man with a gold chain
hanging on his chest, an old woman stands, carrying a filthy
bag. She holds on to the strap with her eyes closed, as if trying
to forget how tired she is.

Kigawa and Yamanaka are in Yada's room. All three are
students at the same university.

"Didn't Koyama get mad at you yesterday?" Yada asks.
Conscious of his friends, he puts on a forced air of intimacy.

"No, not at all," I respond in a similar tone, suppressing my
annoyance. I feel I have no other choice. Kigawa looks sullen
and hasn't said a word since I entered the room. He knew me
well in the old days when I lived with my first love and doesn't
have a good opinion of me. But I like his soft demeanor, which
conceals an icy spot. When he sees me, though, his eyes fill
with hate; he reacts like a man who is forced to look at something festering.

"Since when do you wear frameless glasses?" I ask Yada,
picking them up from a pile of writing paper. "They fit me," I
say, looking up at Kigawa through the glasses, priggishly.

"Let's go. We don't want to be late," says Kigawa, standing
up.

"Oh, are you going somewhere?"

"We're going to the AA Corporation," answers Yada.

"I'll come with you," I say, and before anyone can object, I
stand up, straightening out the skirt of my kimono.

"Why should you go with us?"

"I won't go if you think I'm in the way."

"I didn't say that," Kigawa says, irritated.

The corporation is in Shiba. We take the streetcar to Sudachō where we have to transfer. In the car Yada is pushed by the crowd and gets separated from the rest of us; I stand between Kigawa and Yamanaka.

"Two round trips to Shiba, please," says Kigawa, stretching out his hand to the conductor who comes around behind us. I keep looking straight ahead, pretending that I had not heard Kigawa. He hands one ticket over to Yamanaka behind my back, and still I act as if I'm unaware of what's going on. I will not take money out of my pocket to buy a ticket for myself. As the streetcar approaches Sudachō, Kigawa buys another ticket. He is sneering.

The AA Corporation sets aside a day for the anarchists and revolutionaries who come to them demanding a handout. Several men—one with a beard, another with a walking stick, and the third one in a dirty Russian peasant coat—are waiting their turn near the entrance, they sit around a table which holds a large kettle and several tea cups. One of them hits the table with his Chinese fan, perhaps a demonstration of his determination. When I see the fan, I once again feel ashamed that I'm still wearing my winter kimono.

A young, long-haired receptionist calls out the names. He doesn't look at all like a regular employee and has perhaps been specially hired for the day. The person who is called goes to him, signs a receipt and then goes into the adjacent room to receive the money.

"Five yen? That's not enough. Make them change it to ten yen. They promised me."

"Everybody gets five today, so . . ." the receptionist begins.

"If you're going to insist on five, I'll make you change it to fifteen," the man takes a tea cup from the table and throws it to the floor.

"Stop making such a scene, please. And I hope you won't do this again," the receptionist gives in.

"Next, Ogawa." This is my pseudonym. The men sitting around look at me curiously, surprised to see a woman in such a place.

"Make it ten yen, please."

"I can't. It's five yen today."

"Why did you make it ten for that man over there, then?" I say. Someone mutters words of support for me.

"It's not your own money, is it," I add, feeling encouraged. "This is money extorted from working people. You tell them not to be stingy."

"Please, don't be unreasonable," the receptionist says, but I am able to wangle a receipt for ten yen.

"Not a beauty but she hasn't done badly at all," the man with a Chinese fan says and grins. It was loud enough for me to hear.

When I come out of the room with my ten yen in hand, I first spot Kigawa, who forces a smile. He evidently doesn't want to say anything to the receptionist when his turn comes. He simply nods. None of my companions get more than five yen.

"Women have an advantage after all," says Yada, impressed with my success. When I see Kigawa responding to Yada with the same sardonic smile, I feel insulted and even more rebellious than before. On our way back I talk only to Yada, ignoring the other two completely. Secretly, however, I fret, knowing that I have to tell Yada that I want money.

"What are you going to do now?" Yada asks his friends when we come to the streetcar stop. He makes it clear that he wants to be left alone with me.

"We're going home," Yamanaka says.

"I'll go home, too," I say, on an urge to rebel against Yada. I'm tired of Kigawa's insults. What's between Yada and me is none of his business, I say to myself. A streetcar stops, and just when it is about to leave Kigawa jumps on, without a word. Yamanaka follows him, leaving Yada and me behind. The streetcar picks up speed and disappears into the dusty air.

"Shall we walk?" Yada says. I cannot bear the sight of his dull face, and so instead of responding I look at the display in the store window. Through the dusty window I see a sooty statue of the Hotei Diety and several tea bowls. When I look up, I see my own blackened face reflected in the window. Face powder turned grey, and mostly gone except around the eyes and nose; the tip of the nose shining with grease. Frightened, I turn away and follow Yada.

So I end up in Yada's room after all, unable to decide other-wise. I feel totally miserable as I watch him close the English book he has been studying. He looks like an old man. How did I become this man's lover, I wonder. At the same time, I'm watching for my chance to bring up the promised money. I am so intense that I feel the strain around my eyebrows. Toward evening he suggests that we go to a play performed by a group of his friends.

"Well, if you want to . . ." I say, and am impatient at my inability to talk about the money. Oblivious to my mood, Yada goes to the closet and takes out an early-summer kimono that had been stored away with mothballs. He looks at himself in the mirror and grins. Feeling I have no choice, I decide to go with him.

I cannot find my *geta* at the front door where I had left them earlier. I look around, mumbling. Then I hear a voice saying that they are in Yada's shoe box. "Because I thought you were staying tonight," the voice says sharply. I now notice a small window at the corner of the sliding door dividing the hall and the landlord's room; the voice belongs to the landlady who has been watching us through the window. My worn-out *geta* were placed on top of Yada's, upside down. A shiver goes through my spine the moment I see the two pairs of *geta*. They force me to see my situation very clearly.

It is still light outside and reddish, moist air fills the streets. I think of the room above the barber shop, somewhere way back in the suburbs that stretch beyond the downtown area, and the man I left there, the man who is probably thinking of his woman who has gone out. I cannot supress a feeling of warmth toward that man, although I also feel the satisfaction of revenge.

The play is not bad for a group of amateur actors. "Better than Matsunosuke" is the comment Yada repeats to every ac-quaintance he meets during the intermission. He thinks that his comment is very clever. I cannot totally concentrate on the stage. When the curtain goes down and the bright lights are turned on, I bend down behind the person in front of me; it undoubtedly appears that I am trying to protect my eyes from the bright light but in fact I am looking around carefully in case there is anyone among the audience that I know. I had spotted Kigawa earlier, sitting not too far from me, and that certainly has caused me some confusion. In the last scene of the play the heroine met with her former lover, whom she had not been able to forget. She described her life in one word—"hell"—and fainted. At that moment I suddenly burst out laughing. My state of mind had been unsettled during the play; I hadn't been able to control my tears and had even begun to feel dizzy. When the heroine cried out, it ripped through me like a dagger. My composure disintegrated and I laughed uncontrollably, unable to get a grip on myself.

The play is over and, pushed by the crowd, I reach the door, still undecided whether I want to go back with Yada. The word hell reverberates in my ears. I feel like fainting, like crying out "hell" as the heroine has done on the stage. I walk along in the cold, moist wind and after a while notice Yada walking behind me. He seems to assume that I'm going back to his apartment with him.

"I feel sorry for Koyama," he says abruptly. I feel too weary to respond. Then, beyond the crowd walking away from the theater, I see a black shadow standing with his face toward us. It looks like Koyama.

"Did you come to meet me? How did you know that I was here?" I say, running to him. I forget about Yada at that moment and feel relieved that I am returning to my legitimate place.

"So you went to see a play today?" Koyama says in a hoarse voice, glancing at my face.

The bamboo shoots have grown slender. It is already summer. The fragrance of the passania flowers drifts into my room through the open window. Facing the bamboo field, I sit on the windowsill all day long till my back goes numb; the scent of the flower makes my whole body feel tired. Pregnant, I say to myself. The sensations in my body seem similar to what I've felt before. A child? Now? The mere possibility seems comic, incongruous, and unthinkable.

Weeks pass without my period, and the end of another month is approaching. There isn't even one yen in my wallet. I feel so weary that I can't bring myself even to read a newspaper. Meanwhile the imagined lump in my lower abdomen seems to be growing. Koyama sits on the windowsill whistling a tune. We have only three sen between us, and the rice bag lies in the cupboard, as empty as a dying old man. I am looking down the road where children are playing some kind of game. Among the small children is a husky kid with a torn kimono; he seems to be winning and gaining the cards that had belonged to smaller ones. I see the mailman approaching. It is Koyama, however, who goes down as soon as he hears the mailman's voice downstairs. The mail is a thin poetry magazine published by one of his friends.

"It's near the streetcar station,
and besides there's a nice view;
But your noble wife goes to town and sells mourning bands
Heroically, and with such modest pride."

Koyama reads these lines of verse written by his friend, first to himself, then to me. And then he laughs hysterically.

"He says it well," says Koyama. "The way we live is precisely like selling mourning bands. It's a fine observation."

I grab the magazine, suspecting something. I am right. Yada must have told. I feel my face turn pale.

"'Selling mourning bands' expresses our life so well, don't you think? I've been wanting to describe my feeling about it for some time. But 'Wife goes to town and sells mourning bands' is very good. I'm impressed."

Realizing that Koyama suspects nothing, I turn my face away from the magazine. At that moment I feel a strange sensation in the lower part of my body. In the bathroom I see a dark-colored stream running out of my body. Koyama keeps repeating his praise for "selling mourning bands" for the rest of the day. Each time I hear it I nearly suffocate and feel strangely ticklish. In bed that night I am composed enough to mutter to myself, "I've sold a mourning band." By the time I hear Koyama's heavy breathing next to me, however, I am crying, thrown into a despair that I've never experienced before. My tears trickle down quietly onto the pattern of the quilt.

Original title: *Azakeru* (1927).

Hayashi Fumiko

(1903–1951)

TO EAT AND TO WRITE are the two reasons for living, Hayashi Fumiko once said. Until the time she established herself as a successful writer, the life of Fumiko followed a pattern similar to that of Hirabayashi Taiko and Uno Chiyo: an ambitious young woman, she went to Tokyo seeking better opportunities and spent several years working in poverty, barely surviving from day to day. Though her life was considerably shorter, Fumiko achieved greater fame as a writer than either Taiko and Chiyo. She was the first woman fiction writer in modern Japan who enjoyed both popular success and critical recognition; she was able to compete effectively with men and fared well in male-dominated literary circles. During her twenty-year career she produced an enormous amount of work, including poems, short stories, and novels, many of which were important for their fine artistic quality as well as for their immense popularity. *Vagabond's Song* (*Hōrō-ki*), a novel that established her reputation as a writer, sold over 600,000 copies and inspired three films; nine of her other novels also became films. Fumiko continued to write with remarkable intensity until the day of her death at age forty-eight. Her prodigious output totaled some 30,000 pages, which she left behind in two hundred and seventy-eight books.

How to survive and get ahead in life were lessons Fumiko learned at an early age, while wandering from town to town with her mother and stepfather. Her stepfather, an incompetent but amiable man who treated Fumiko kindly, was a peddler. During her childhood Fumiko had to change primary schools seven times and sometimes had long periods of absence. Still, when she was fifteen she enrolled herself in high school and completed the four-year course by working at night in the factories and as a maid during school vacations. Unable to help her financially, Fumiko's mother did support her by insisting that the family not move again until Fumiko finished high school. With the exception of creative writing, Fumiko was not a very good student, but she was an avid reader and spent much of her time alone, reading the work of many writers including Western authors such as Whitman and Heine. The exposure to world literature provided her with inspiration for her own writing later.

The rootlessness of her childhood and adolescence was often the subject of Fumiko's early pieces. "The Town with the Hand Organ and the Fish" (*Fūkin to Uo no Machi*, 1931), for example, draws on her days of moving from one cheap inn to another, dramatically conveying the poverty of her childhood. Fumiko's mother, Kiku, who lived to see her daughter's glorious days of success, had a lasting influence on her daughter. An unconventional woman, Kiku bore several children by different lovers— including Fumiko, who was registered by her father as "illegitimate"—before marrying Fumiko's stepfather. Her warmth and carefree nature, characteristic of the people of her native island Kyūshū, was a source of comfort and peace to Fumiko. She maintained a close and loving relationship with her mother throughout her life and as an adult often returned to her mother's town in southern Japan to replenish her inner resources and nourish her sturdy optimism.

Unlike Hirabayashi Taiko, Fumiko had no revolutionary ideals when she went to Tokyo in the spring of 1922; nor did she have clearly defined literary aspirations. It is said that she went there in search of a man whom she had known since high school and hoped to marry. She found him, a university student, and they lived together briefly. Her lover gave her up in the face of strong objections from his family, a betrayal that temporarily devastated her. In order to survive, Fumiko took any job she could find—she worked as a clerk, a waitress, a salesperson and even a checkgirl for shoes at a public bathhouse. Forced to change jobs and locations frequently, perhaps due to her volatile temperament as well as the need to earn better wages, Fumiko lived on the fringes of society and accumulated a great deal of firsthand knowledge of the people who shared her existence. This proved to be a rich resource for her writing.

Fumiko started writing poetry and found it a natural and spontaneous way of expressing herself. Eventually she found a woman friend who also wrote poetry, and with twenty yen from an anarchist student acquaintance (who happened to be from a rich family), they published a tabloid entitled *Two of Us* (*Futari*). The publication of Fumiko's first book, a collection of poems entitled *I Saw a Blue Horse* (*Sōma o Mitari*, 1929), was also financed by a donation from a friend.

During this period Fumiko lived with and financially supported an abusive man who selfishly kept his own private savings account and carried on a secret love affair. She finally left him and moved in with a poor art student, Tezuka Ryokutoshi. Ryokutoshi proved to be an ideal partner for Fumiko, not only as a stabilizing factor in her personal life but also as a sustaining and supporting force in her professional life as a writer. He was a generous man, often putting his wife's needs ahead of his own. Ryokutoshi later adopted Fumiko's family name of Hayashi, a demonstration of his broadmindedness and a recognition of her status. Fumiko and Ryokutoshi maintained a happy relationship throughout their life together, from early days of poverty to later years of wealth.

In 1928, *Women and the Arts* (*Nyonin Geijitsu*), a literary magazine produced by women, began publication. This was a significant turning point for Fumiko and other women who had been writing but had been unable to find publishers for their work. The magazine quickly became an important forum for aspiring writers. Fumiko's *Vagabond's Song*, which had been rejected by commercial publishers, found its first welcome in the journal, where it was serialized. Among the readers of *Women and the Arts* was an influential editor who recognized Fumiko's talent and sought her out. (Although Fumiko would make a small fortune within a few years, she was so poor at the time of this editor's visit that she greeted him in her bathing suit, the only clothing she had to wear.)

The editor published *Vagabond's Song* in book form in 1930, and it became an immediate success.

The novel is both a collection of sketches of daily incidents, in the manner of impressionist watercolors, and a journal of a young woman, who is poor but full of dreams and the courage to resist the drudgery of a non-creative life. Clearly autobiographical, the story describes the cafés and other places where Fumiko had worked; the streets, the women with whom she had shared small rooms, the men who had caused her pain, and her mother, portrayed as living in a remote southern town but always present in the mind of the narrator. The writing is characterized by a free-flowing, poetic sensibility that many readers had not seen before in fiction written by women, and its readability contributed to the book's great popularity. The novel was also unique in that it depicted café life from the point of view of the women who worked there. The café had become a vital part of city life in Japan in the 1920s; like the geisha houses decades earlier, cafés—along with dance halls and bars—sprang up in the large cities, symbols of developing mass culture amidst spreading economic hardship. The vagabond narrator of Fumiko's novel was an appealing character and readers empathized with her struggles to overcome her bleak existence. Fumiko later acknowledged the key role Knut Hamsun's book, *Hunger*, had played in the conception of *Vagabond's Song*. Like the narrator of *Hunger*, the protagonist of Fumiko's novel transcends despair, turning misery into aspiration.

The commercial success of *Vagabond's Song* established Hayashi Fumiko as a highly marketable author in the minds of publishers, but she also achieved critical recognition. At the end of the following year, 1931, she wrote a short piece, entitled "The Poor" (*Seihin no Sho*), describing her life with Ryokutoshi. This work received rave notices from the critics and gained her membership among the writers of so-called pure literature. Fumiko was greatly encouraged by this but realized that she could not limit her creative writing to the portrayal of poverty and its victims. Although many of her stories are autobiographical, Fumiko proved she also could create characters and situations for which she had no living model. "The Oyster" (*Kaki*, 1935) is about a feeble-minded and neurotic craftsman who is slowly going mad. "The Crested Ibis" (*Toki*, 1935) portrays a diligent and kind-hearted young woman who feels she will not be able to marry because of a birthmark on her face. Fumiko was a dedicated and hard-working artist, and one of the few women writers of her day who dealt aggressively with male publishers and editors and used her popularity to her own advantage.

Despite her association with anarchist and socialist friends, Fumiko never allied herself with a proletarian school of writing. A born realist who learned early to deal with hard reality, she was never lured by revolutionary idealism. She grew and developed as a writer by reading vociferously and by traveling widely to see people and places. Her trips began in the 1930s and she continued to travel consistently until she died. In 1931 she went to Paris and stayed a year and a half, reading and taking in the opera, plays and art museums. She financed the trip by writing essays and a travel journal. It was not easy to live in France at that time, as francs were very expensive, and when she returned to Japan in 1933, she was suffering from malnutrition. Fumiko also made several trips to China, where she met Lu Hsun, a writer well-known in Japan. In the year following the outbreak of the China Incident of 1937, she traveled to visit soldiers as a part of "the pen squadron"—writers recruited by the military authorities to travel to the front-lines—and she was the first Japanese woman to see the battle-front at Nanking and Kangchow. Her masterpiece novel, *The Floating Cloud* (*Ukigumo*, 1949-50, tr. 1965), is based on her travels to Southeast Asia during the war years and is the story of a young woman and a man who have both been spiritually devastated by the war. *The Floating Cloud* is the best among the very few works of fiction that portray the confusion, apathy and moral despair suffered by the Japanese people in the post-war period. Fumiko's friend and rival, Hirabayashi Taiko, remarked that even had she written nothing else, Fumiko's name would be imprinted in modern Japanese literature as the author of *The Floating Cloud*. The novel demonstrated that Fumiko was capable of writing a full-length novel with complex characterization, sustained plot development and large social perspectives, an achievement only one or two Japanese women writers had accomplished before her.

Except during the last four years of World War II, when physical survival was everyone's immediate concern, Fumiko wrote enough stories to have them compiled into an average of four or five books a year; within the first two years after the war she published eleven books. The thematic thread woven through all of her books is the many ways in which women, young, old and middle-aged, live their lives—whether struggling against or resigning themselves to their fate. Many of Fumiko's stories dealt with relatively unexplored aspects of women's existence, describing the lives of prostitutes and other women shunned by society, as well as more traditional women bound to their men through sexual desire. One of her finest stories, "The Late Chrysanthemum" (*Bangiku*, 1948, tr. 1960), portrays a lonely middle-aged woman, once a geisha and now the proprietress of a successful restaurant, who has been deeply disillusioned by men.

Fumiko died in 1951 at the peak of her career. Vast numbers of people came to mourn her death, so many that traffic policemen were needed to assist the crowds attending the funeral. People from the publishing world were joined by many ordinary women, young and not-so-young, with aprons and shopping bags. It is interesting to compare this public display of emotion and respect with the funeral of another major woman writer, Higuchi Ichiyō, held half a century earlier, where only ten mourners attended. It is perhaps an indication of the tremendous advances made in the status of female artists during the first half of the twentieth century.

Fumiko was among the first writers to respond to the needs of modern Japan's widened audience. Her writing never lost the down-to-earth sensibility and sense of immediacy that won so many new readers, and her vivid style and probing themes make her fiction among the most significant and lasting in modern Japanese literature.

Y. T.

Vagabond's Song

translated by Elizabeth Hanson

A song of sorrow
Becomes a song
Of mere smoke

Women are tossed about like flags in a breeze, I think as I wait in this long line. These women around me wouldn't be here if their circumstances were better. It is their need for work that binds them.

Unemployment is an assault, your life becomes confused like that of an unchaste woman. What does it mean, that I can't get a job that pays a mere thirty yen per month? With five yen I could buy some good quality Akita rice. I would cook it to the right fluffiness and eat it with *takuan* pickles. This is all I ask. Can't something be done for me?

The line grows shorter; some come out of the door smiling, others look disappointed. Those of us still waiting by the door gradually become irritable. More than a hundred of us are waiting to apply for two jobs available at this wholesale grain store. Finally it is my turn. In comparing our qualifications, the employer looks first at appearance, build, and weight. Exposed to stares for a few moments, I am told I will be notified by mail. I'm used to this procedure, but still, it's distasteful. How unfortunate that I was born. If one is exceptionally beautiful, that is fortune enough. I have nothing. Nothing except this strong body.

I always fail miserably at making a living, this most important of human occupations. I'm like a cheap ready-made dress, bound to fall apart. The boss has very keen eyes. He won't hire a woman like me.

But if I were to get the job, I'd work so hard for my thirty yen a month that I'd cough blood. I'm tired of spending evenings working at that stall. I'm truly sick of it. I'm tired of breathing dust, I'm tired of looking up at people standing in front of me, I'm tired of forcing smiles. It's humiliating. More than anything I want to go to huge Russia. Hey, Mr. Barin, Barin. Russia is much, much larger than Japan. How pleasant it must be, if it's a country with fewer women than men.

I'll buy some ink on my way home.

"I would like very much to see you.

"How I would like some money.

"Even ten yen would be most adequate.

"I long to eat a bowl of Chinese noodles.

"I want to visit the theater.

"I'd love to go to Korea, even to Manchuria, to work.

"It would be wonderful to see you, even once.

"And I truly would like some money."

I wrote to him, but nothing will come of it. He's already married. To console myself I compose some lyrics to a song.

Nighttime.

I can't sleep, so I turn on the light and read a tattered copy of Eugene O'Neill. The landlord, who is a carpenter, works late into the night with his lathe, making toy tops out of wood. In this world we all must work day and night in order to eat. The mosquitoes buzz noisily but I can't afford a mosquito net. I try burning a heap of sawdust on a plate to get rid of them. Hardy mosquitoes, noisy mosquitoes. I wish I could buy my mother new summer kimono, but I can't.

August—.

A bright day. The trees around the Junija Shintō shrine are a blinding green. A man leads the shrine horse, unsaddled, around the pond. The horse, covered with sweat, looks like velvet. The cries of cicadas rise.

The banner in front of the shaved ice shop doesn't stir.

Mother and I walk along with bundles on our backs. It's dreadfully hot. Summer in Tokyo is stifling.

We walk to Shinjuku to save streetcar fare and then buy five skewers of grilled dumplings from a place called Miyoshino in Narukozaka. Drinking cup after cup of tea, for a few moments I feel content.

O'Neill was a nameless sailor, who spent his time wandering; as a child he was incorrigible, and as an adult he boarded a ship bound for Buenos Aires and led a life full of adventure. After he became famous, such tales of his life didn't sound particularly strange. Maybe I will write a play. A fantastic, highly original play. Or perhaps a sad one. I wonder if O'Neill was always tragically sad.

No doubt there were times when he felt happy enough to hum a tune to himself.

Staggering under her load, the pretty little thing walks the streets of the hot city. I don't care what happens. I'm desperate. My shadow, reflected sharply on the street, creeps along like a toad.

Why did my poor mother give birth to me? It doesn't matter that I'm illegitimate, that's not my mother's fault. How can I blame her? You find illegitimate children no matter where you go in the world. That's the way life is. Women live to have children. They don't worry about formalities. If a woman likes a man, she surrenders her body to him.

At a barbershop at Kagurazaka I'm given a drink of water.

Today is the temple festival. I should be busy at the stall this evening.

I watch groups of pretty geisha pass; the man who sells *shinobu* grass and the goldfish vendor are setting up their stands. Today I have a spot next to a woman who sells those paper flowers that expand when you put them in a glass of water.

After setting up my stall, I sit on a mat under an umbrella. A blazing sunset. Where does it come from, I wonder? Heat like a sizzling calm on an ocean. A ridiculous number of people are passing by this evening, but it doesn't look like I'll sell many pairs of socks or underwear. Mother has gone on an errand to Shitaya.

In front of a hardware stall, a man has put out his checkered awning and is selling fancy beetles that children like to keep in little bamboo cages. A vendor of Chinese medicine passes.

A man in a cotton kimono, a towel around his neck, rides his bicycle down the sloping street, holding a polished wooden box with handles.

Scenes of a bustling city—no one pays any attention to a lone woman crouched below an umbrella.

> The devil's tongue is the crimson sunset
> Sunk in the boiling sky
> The shape of his nose, full of sorrow,
> The glitter that sparks beyond it
> I don't wish to live,
> Simply to exist, not bothering anyone
> From the hazy path in the realm of the dead
> Signs of being or not-being
> I wasn't prepared for my youth, it was all guessing
> And now it has rotted into ashes
> Tell me the truth,
> This is all I want.
> In the subhuman dust,
> In the miniature world of a rainbow,
> Snails topple
> They become the dew on each blade of grass
> Then they fade.
> Playing such evil tricks is a useless way to live
> In the bloodless world of snails.
> Oh the world of dreams
> I curse the rich people of that world
> The wonder of the blazing evening sun
> That has no beginning.

Sitting beneath my umbrella, so dry that it rustles, I gaze at the red setting sun.

September—.

Entering a café and seeing the containers of smudged chopsticks, I feel my poverty. With a pair of balding lacquer chopsticks that have touched the mouths of other people, I eat my rice. It's exactly like being a dog. I no longer notice the dirtiness. I don't feel like a human being. I bite into a grilled sardine, lost in the sensation of its intense deliciousness and in the aroma of the small dish of cooked greens.

I will always feel insecure. Even though I creep about like a dog, even though I sometimes wish I could die, even though I wish sometimes I could cheat someone, I don't have the strength. My cuffs and collar are worn to a shine. I'd rather go about naked.

I leave the café and go to the publishing house at Dōzaka. When I see the crowd of people milling around on the other side of the dilapidated wall, I hesitate. This publishing house is a nest of fleas. It has nothing to do with culture, it's nothing but a building surrounded by a rickety fence. I begin to think that my manuscript about a wandering minstrel of a woman, the manuscript I worked on all night long, will never earn me any money. I don't think I can ever write a story like those by that popular writer, Namiroku.

You see, I don't have enough money to pay my rent; for the last two or three days I have done my best not to eat any meals at my boarding house. Even though I don't know how to write popular stories, I took Namiroku as my example and wrote until my eyes were bloodshot, but in the end this doesn't earn me a cent. A red mail truck passes. It seems a good omen. There must be piles of envelopes with cash inside. I don't know who they are from or who they are going to, but I wonder if just one or two might fly out and land in front of me.

I go to another publishing house, this one in Koishikawa.

The gate looks like it belongs to a samurai's mansion; I expect a doorman to appear. The building looks like a haunted house. I'm led to a tatami room that reminds me of the waiting room in a country doctor's office. Weary-looking people are sitting about, waiting. They stare at me when I come into the room; they must think it strange to see me here because I look like a young girl. These people wouldn't believe that I have written a story about a wandering minstrel woman.

I like the name Ichiyō, "One Leaf," very much. I also like Ozaki Kōyō. Oguri Fūyō is good too. All the famous writers use the character for "leaf" somewhere in their pen names; I should try to use "five leaves" somewhere in my name when I write stories. A tall man in a faded kimono comes from the office into the waiting room. My heart beats faster. I wish I hadn't come. He tells me he will give me an answer after he has read my work, and I hand my pitiful manuscript over to a complete stranger. Quickly I leave and take a deep breath. In spite of everything, I am still alive! Please, don't torment me more than necessary. Oh God! I could care less about men. It's money that I want so badly. I wonder which part of town the moneylenders live in. I walk to the botanical gardens.

A lovely sunset. The autumn sun sinks quickly. I too tumble to the ground. The fireworks of melancholy daydreams. I realize how silly this business of storytelling is.

Underneath a tree an old woman wearing a straw hat is painting a picture. Her work is quite good. I watch her for a moment, smelling the rich aroma of the oil paints. I wonder if this woman has enough to eat. The painting is of children playing on the grass. There's not a child anywhere in the park, but two children are crouching in this painting. I would like to try being a painter myself.

I lie down beneath a bush clover that is filled with white blossoms. Picking a blade of grass, I chew on it and feel a simple contentment. Gradually the sunset deepens.

Although I've never thought of my life in terms of happiness or unhappiness, for this one moment I am happy. My eyes fill with tears as I lie quietly on my stomach on the grass. Tears are nothing but a kind of water, but even so, they make me feel lonelier. The life I'm living now is not unbearably difficult, but it's hard not to be able to pay my rent. Even if the sky has no bounds, we human beings still must toil away.

How sad that there can be no miracle in a small human life like the miracle of the blazing sunset. Suddenly I find myself thinking of my former lover. I often thought him a horrible person, but now I don't; I've forgotten all the things I didn't like about him.

Right now the sweet white bush clover is blooming, but sooner or later winter will come, and the flowers and the stems will dry up. Just wait and see. The relationship between men and women is like this, I guess. Namiroku says in her novel *Cuckoo* that she wanted to live a thousand or ten thousand years, but how little she knew about human life! A flower blooms and falls in a year's time, human beings live fifty years at most. How depressing it is.

I imagine appealing directly to the Emperor. I dream that he will take a fancy to me and ask me to go away with him. In dreams we human beings have our last freedom. I would serve the Emperor some chilled sake and other delicacies; he would surely pronounce them delicious. Why was I born in Japan? They say there is a place called Sicily where people love music. I'd like to see what Sicilians are like.

Suddenly an evening cicada begins to cry. The sunset gradually grows strangely pale.

September—.

Morning comes but nothing has changed.

Last night I decided to try to sell my futon bedding, and relieved, I slept well. But today is so cool, I can't think of selling it. My life is like one of those novels by Kasai Zenzō where there is nothing but poverty. I don't have any desire to drink sake, but I can't go on living this way.

I'd like to eat some pickled scallions and some sweet beans. I'd also like to buy some benzine to clean the stains on my kimono. I hear a student coming home from a night on the town, his slippers flapping on the stairs. From here to the Yoshiwara Quarters is not far. I wonder how much a woman costs there.

In the morning, I have to prepare for my day. A sparrow is chirping. A clear sky. The leaves of the persimmon tree peek through the window. Someone in the kitchen is singing in a small voice. For a moment I consider taking a job as a maid in this boarding house, which would mean nothing more than moving down from a guest room to a maid's room. I wouldn't need a salary. Food and shelter would be enough. The student in the English Department of the Imperial University who stayed in this room before I came scratched something into the wall with a knife: "Where is the Garden of Eden?" I don't know, either. Apparently this young snob flunked out of school and went back to his hometown. I have no hometown to return to.

Dadaist poetry is popular now; I find it boring and childish, a game with words. No blood flows in it. There is no self-abandoned honesty, only despair. When I try to compose such poetry, I close my eyes and come up with a poem about a parasol and a bird. When my eyes are closed, images fly from the darkness, one after the other. I think only of strange things. First, I remember fragrances. Then I feel my nose filling with watery tears. Then comes a soundless shriek as if a crocodile has sunk his teeth into me. My breasts feel heavy, and I topple with their weight like a sack of flour. A white star appears in my fingernail. They say there are good omens, but I don't believe it. I sleep on a dank mattress that hasn't been covered with a sheet for ages. This is truly the Garden of Eden. The quilt is made from an old theater banner, a stained canvas bed.

> *Someone, someone just out of the reformatory*
> *Calls "Forgive me" again and again*
> *"Please" and "Thank you"*
> *A beggar standing in the rain*
> *A moan of despair*
> *No contact with anyone on earth*
>
> *Fumiko, who's been in the reformatory*
> *Is an inhuman chunk of ice*

The sweetness of old Japanese words
I'm dizzy
The journey is dangerous
What did you say?

A reformatory, set up by a government
The Imperial University, set up by the government.
There is little difference.

October—.

I visit my friend Shizue Tomodani at her boarding house in
Dangozaka. We talk about starting a literary magazine called
Futari, "Two of Us." I am uneasy about this plan, unable to
raise even ten yen myself, but surely Shizue would help in
some way. The lives of rich people seem so mysterious to me,
I don't know what to say.

On Tomodani's invitation we go together to the public
bath. Our two small naked bodies are reflected in the morning
light of the mirror. We look like sculpture by Maillol, two
frolicking cats. For no specific reason, I long to go to a foreign
country. A place like India, where people walk about with
piles of bananas on their heads, would be fine. I want to go
somewhere far away. I wonder if I could become a woman
sailor, or if I could work as a nurse on a foreign ship.

I write poems, but I won't be a success. I will starve and
shrivel up. I wonder if my life would be easier if I were beautiful . . . Tomodani is a pretty woman. She radiates self-confidence. Her skin is dark, but has the aroma of wild fruit. My
naked body looks like a plump boy's. Nothing but fat. My
large buttocks are a sign of being low class. I don't eat a lot of
rich food, but still I gain weight. I'm rolling with fat.

Tomodani dusts the nape of her neck with thick white powder. Her dark skin grows pale as a cloud. I haven't used powder for a long time; I stand in front of the mirror like a boy and
start to do calisthenics. How funny it would be to run out the
door just as I am and walk to the main road.

"Starting off naked on a journey . . ." There was a song to
this effect, but if no one says they like me, I think I could stand

naked in front of that man and cry . . .

On the way back from the public bath, Tomodani and I stop
at a noodle shop. The fragrance of the *nori* seaweed on the cold
buckwheat noodles is wonderful. The weather is fine, with a
clear sky. In the garden by the shop, I notice the head of a large
white chrysanthemum, supported with a paper collar as thin
as *somen* noodles. Such large flowers look abnormal . . . Nothing is better than eating noodles after a bath. We decide to
publish five hundred copies of the magazine, which should
cost eighteen yen. It would be eight pages long, printed on
good quality paper. I consider pawning one of my good kimonos. Surely I could get four or five yen for it.

To write. Only that. To lose myself in my writing. It's pho-
ny to pose as a European poet. I can forget the posing. When
I'm hungry, I'll write that I'm hungry. When I'm in love, I'll
write that I'm in love. Isn't this enough?

To deceive no one, to say the sky is beautiful, that plates are
pretty, with nothing but exclamatory words. I'll try to write a
genuine Dadaist poem.

On the way back we meet Gojuzato Kōtarō. The hem of his
kimono is tucked up to the hip even though it is cool, a serge
kimono with a sash. I'm not interested in going home, so we
leave Dōzaka and walk toward Sendagichō. Some street musi-
cians walk along the pleasantly cool road. Then we go toward
the First High School. The leaves of the gingko trees on the
grounds of the Imperial University are gold. We turn at the
Enrakukan Restaurant and try to find a hotel called Kikufuji. I
heard that a writer named Uno Kōji has been staying there for
some time now. I'm a bit in awe of novelists, they are not at all
like poets. I'm afraid that he might say something cruel, but
still, I'd like to meet him.

They say Uno used to write his stories while lying in bed. I
wonder if he was an invalid. It's difficult to lie down and write
at the same time. I find the hotel without trouble. Trembling, I
go in, and the maid leads me cheerfully to the room. Uno slept
under a pale green quilt. No doubt he is the type who writes
while lying down. He has long sideburns like a Spaniard. I feel
that the room of a novelist conveys a kind of contentment.

"Try to write as you speak," he said. But deep down I don't think this is possible. A cluttered room. Someone else comes and I leave quickly. I have a long way to go to reach Uno. I like his name. It isn't easy to write while reclining. Writing as one speaks is a problem. When I try to write, "Um, well," it doesn't work.

There is something unsettling about a writer's room. As I walk along, the long purple skirts of the women art students passing me give off a pleasant fragrance. Novels may be tedious. The people around me walk, speak and live with energy. Walking along the streets is more interesting than reading a novel.

Nighttime. I return to my boarding house.

A note from Nomura is waiting, asking me to visit on Sunday. I sit in my bare room, unable to relax. Following Uno's example, I imagine lying down to write, but I know that if I try to support my fat body on my elbows, they'll fall asleep. The boarding house is noisy at dinnertime. The aroma of the food that others are able to buy makes me envious.

December—.

I go out with Yoshi, who is carrying her baby on her back, into the snow that has been falling steadily since morning. It looks as if the snow will pile up, but it melts with surprising speed. On the way to Kaneiji Slope, we meet Kyōjiro. He says he is staying at a friend's place, and walks on with two men I've never met.

He's a handsome man, and honest. But I don't understand his poetry at all. When I see him, I think immediately of Okamoto. I like Okamoto. I can't help but be disappointed that Tomodani is his wife. Men don't care for women like me.

It's so cold that we buy some pancakes from a stand in front of a temple and walk along eating them. The last two we divide between us and hold underneath our kimonos against our skin.

"Oh, it's hot," Yoshi says, laughing.

I put mine against my stomach. My skin is permeated with

the pleasant warmth, as if I am holding a pocket-sized hand
warmer. My unbearable loneliness seems to be scorching inside me. Snow falls on Kaneiji Slope. Climbing the steep
street, we go under the bridge near Uguisudani Station, and
on to the employment agency at Kappazaka, where I applied
earlier. I'm best suited for two jobs, one as a maid in an inn at
Inage and one as a servant at a butcher's shop in Asakusa.

Yoshi says she will take the child and go to the inn at Inage,
and I decide to go to Asakusa. It seems unnecessary for her to
take a job in a faroff place like Inage, but she appears peculiarly
attached to the idea, saying that a job near the sea would be
good for the child, who has asthma. The child is illegitimate;
she says the father is a member of the House of Representa-
tives. I don't know if this is true or not. It seems unlikely that
the homely Yoshi would know such a man, and if she did,
there would be no need for her to go off to work in Inage.

Paying the three-yen fee, I feel I've been cheated. Fortunately I didn't have to give the name of a reference.

At a used book store in Asakusa, I find an old literary magazine. I note a yellowed ad for a book called *Above the Earth* by a
nineteen-year-old genius, Shimada Seijirō. Nineteen is probably a good age for a prodigy ... I always dream of being a
genius, but I'm distracted with thoughts of being hungry and
will end up being mediocre.

January—.

A clear, crisp day. The snow is almost blinding. A woman
in her forties sits on her bed, enjoying a cigarette. The cotton
quilt, which has no cover, looks greasy. The walls are covered
with newspaper, the tatami mats are balding and yellowed,
the ceiling is stained. Melting snow runs in the gutters. If I
listen carefully, the snow dripping from the eaves sounds like
the beats of a festival drum. Everyone is up, transients getting
themselves ready for the day. I open the window, reach out
and take a handful of snow from the roof, then wash my face
with it. I put some cold cream on my face, then rub two circles
of powder into my cheeks. My hair I arrange so that my cov-

ered ears look like small dumplings. I feel itchy around my ears.

A bird is singing. The railroad tracks vibrate. In the morning the streets are a mass of mud. Even so, everyone is alive, this poor part of town where people imagine setting off on journeys.

The woman in her thirties who slept beside me has a silver watch. Last night she told me again and again about how well-off she once was. Now her purple velveteen *tabi* socks are filthy and torn.

Mother and I have three useless bundles wrapped in scarves. Without any particular goal in mind, I leave Tamaga. This cheap boarding house has become my haven, my Palermo.

The brilliance of wide open spaces. Nothing is obscure. Only my heart is heavy as I go out into the slushy, muddy streets. The telephone poles, like thin crucifixes, shine in the sunlight. These poles and the streets are all convenient companions for travelling into degradation. I'm tired of this life of nakedness. Perhaps I should throw myself at the car of some rich aristocrat and then I'll be summoned to him . . . How lonely it is to be young. There's nothing so great about it . . . My hands are swollen like dumplings. At the base of my fingers are dimples. When I was in school, the teacher called these my "dimpled hands." Smiling hands. Even now my hands are smiling.

Doesn't anyone have a use for a girl who looks as if she just came from a mountain village? There is no point in asking for an advance from houses in the red-light district.

I leave Mother at our lodgings and set off into the muddy streets, going from café to café. In the morning the back entrances are dirty and depressing. Courage, courage, I tell myself, but it doesn't help. I decide to take a job at a rundown place called the Golden Star, better suited to a name like "Star of Hades." Here, I'll set off fireworks. Nearby is a group of brothels; they say the café does a good business. A little girl in the kitchen gives me a cracker. I feel tears well suddenly in my eyes. At a shop I buy a pair of new *tabi* socks for fifteen sen.

Our room costs thirty-five sen apiece. Since we were able to pay seventy sen in advance, I feel secure there. I buy an order of fried oysters and white rice to share with mother.

That evening I go to work at the Golden Star. Myself included, there are three waitresses. I'm the youngest. I wonder if I can find my Nevrodov. If I try to look agreeable and carefree, I should be able to earn some decent tips, even if I am a bit plump. I'm as determined as most bargirls. Ah, what is a tip, anyway? No different from begging. A transaction that requires you to look agreeable with all your body, all your strength. How far I am from making my living with my writing. In the dark, stinky bathroom, I stick my tongue out, saying I can't see any longer. I have no hope of writing anything. I can't do anything. Writing poetry is complete foolishness. What about Baudelaire? Heine's big, loose necktie was only a decoration. I wonder how those two managed to make a living.

"Nous avons, vous avez. Pardon, monsieur." This means something like "Please excuse me." Isn't that right?

I leave my kimono jacket with the landlady and borrow two yen. One yen, fifty sen I give to Mother, then I go to the public bath on the main street. Looking in the mirror at myself, I see first a healthy child. My skin is plump and pink, nothing like an adult's. From my neck up I look as if I have a kettle on my head. Waitresses come swarming in, chatting with each other. The bathhouse attendant is busily massaging a woman's shoulders. I notice a painting of a waterfall and posters advertising face powder and obstetricians. It has been so many days since I've taken a bath, it feels strange.

The dim neon signs look out of place in the snowy streets. For my pen name, should I try Yodogimi? Or Kōmori no Yasu? I imagine the stage of Sadanji in the play *Kirihitoha*. Tokyo is a place where many things happen. Even though these are mostly painful, fortunately I forget them quickly. I'll call myself Yumiko, which means Miss Archer. A bow is tough, a consolation. Please hit right on the mark.

A strange customer gives me two yen. An auspicious occasion. At a used book stall beside the muddy road I spend fifty sen on a book of memoirs by Tolstoy and Chekhov. These were published on March 18, 1924. I wonder if I too could write such a book . . .

"I believe that anyone who writes stories must know the beginning and the end. We novelists are excellent liars. And one must be brief. As brief as possible . . ." Chekhov wrote this.

By eleven o'clock there are no customers in the café. As I sit reading in a corner, the big woman, Katsumi, says "You're nearsighted, aren't you?" The other waitress is Oshin. She has two children and commutes back and forth from the shop. Katsumi has dark skin and so rubs it with peroxide. I have decided not to use face powder. I have no interest at all in tampering with my face. Katsumi is the only waitress who boards at the café. This morning, the little girl who gave me the cracker came to the shop, wearing a muslin vest. A thin, sickly child.

Katsumi asks me if I want to go to a circus the next day at Taisōji Temple. There is supposed to be a freak show as well.

I return to the boarding house at two a.m., exhausted. The same lodgers are here tonight.

Unable to sleep, I read by the small lamp beside my pillow.

January—.

I'm amazed. The writer Tolstoy was a count. "Tolstoy's anarchism was expressed principally through our Slavic-style anti-patriotism. This is in fact a national characteristic that has been in our bones since ancient times. It also expresses our desire to wander." I didn't know until today that Tolstoy, that writer who is a great Russian hero, was a count. Even so, he died like a beggar.

Mother, the Russian Tolstoy was a nobleman. I'm shocked. I feel strange, my whole body grows cold.

"Looks like a difficult book you're reading." The woman with the silver watch laughs while she does her hair.

I truly have learned something. I'm shocked to discover that Tolstoy was a nobleman. I'm not interested in Tolstoy's religious affectations, but his art stirs me with its beauty. Tolstoy, you must have been secretly eating fine food. *Anna Karenina*,

Resurrection, such unbearable greatness . . .

Reluctantly, I leave for the Golden Star.

When I think of my former lover, the memories are dim, as small as a grain of sesame. If I had thirty yen I'd like to try to write something long. I wonder if some money might fall from the heavens . . . I wouldn't mind sleeping for one night like a pig in a pigsty. Isn't there anyone who will give me thirty yen?

I dust the tabletops and the chair legs. Ah, such meaningless work. Next I fetch some water and wash the brass fittings on the door. These tasks become unbearable. My hands are purplish and swollen. My "dimpled hands" weep. The little girl plays a tune on a flute. Some prostitutes file past the shop. They look strange, their faces peaked, only the napes of their necks covered with white powder. Their hair is pulled up on their heads in a traditional style. In their long *haori* jackets, they look like country women. No one pays any attention to this procession.

Today I buy an apron edged with lace. The trademark of a waitress. It cost eighty sen.

A freezing day suited to songs about the sadness of Tokyo. My feet are so cold that I decide not to go to the bath but sit on a chair and read. It's really very cold. The new smell of the apron sickens me.

Nighttime.

It's my turn to wait on a group of four or five men who look like construction workers.

Cutlets, fried oysters, fried rice, and some ten bottles of sake. One of the men vomits and starts to cry, others begin to quarrel. I find it quite interesting to sit quietly and watch them. After an hour has passed, they leave for the brothels.

Ah, the world is a big place. I feel sorry for the women who have to service these men. I'm glad I didn't go to one of the houses in the red-light district. I think of the procession of girls who have been procured from the countryside.

Katsumi is rather drunk and has started to sing. She has two customers. Both are imposing in their large overcoats. Oshin chews on a piece of dried squid while she changes the records.

Because business has been good tonight, the owner brings out the hibachi brazier from the back room to supply some heat.

One of Katsumi's customers offers me some sake. It doesn't taste good at all. I drink five or six cups. I'm not the least bit drunk. The older customer with glasses asks me, "Are you seventeen?" I don't feel like smiling but I do. I don't like myself for acting this way.

At eight o'clock, eating my meal of cooked squid, I wonder what *he* is eating now, and I feel lonely. I imagine him a fine man without a fault. A few days after we parted, I had completely forgotten the misery of our life together. I want to write him a loving letter and perhaps enclose a small sum of money.

After the café closes at one a.m., some customers remain.

Katsumi is very drunk, singing a strange song about "Where did I come from, where am I going and at what time?" The small shop is filled with cigarette smoke. Taxi drivers and flower sellers come and go. I want to scream like a crazy person. Katsumi is drunk and emptying fried rice into the hibachi. There is the stench of hot grease.

I return to the boarding house at 2:30.

Tonight the old woman isn't there, instead a couple with their children. I've earned three yen, eight sen. My filthy *tabi* socks feel uncomfortable.

I bring the lamp to my bedside and read. I can't sleep.

We should write of simple things. Certainly it's enough that Peter Semonovich marries Marie Ivanovich. And why should we add sections on psychological analysis, description, and peculiarities? These are simply lies. The title should be as simple as possible, whatever comes naturally to mind, nothing else will do. One should avoid as much as possible parentheses, italics, and hyphens. All of these are trite.

I agree. I feel this way too, but because I am young, the curious, however inappropriate, has charm. Sooner or later, I shall try to emulate Chekhov. Sooner or later.

Memories whirl onto my tablet. They flow with a rumbling noise. In the end I can't write a thing because of my yearnings. If I go on like this, I won't be able to establish myself. I can't imagine being a waitress into my old age. I suppose I'll have to implore God for help. Wanting to write something, I take out my notebook, but as I grip my pencil, not a word comes to mind. I'm preoccupied with thoughts of my former lover.

I can't think about the future; it's like a dream. I wonder if I should write a story that records exactly what I'm thinking.

Mother says she wants to go back to the country. She's absolutely right. I too would like to go back and breathe the fresh country air, but I can't with the wretched wages I earn now.

February—.

> *The morning mist is whiter than a ship*
> *A transparent stone of faraway tears*
> *Stones buried in the cruel earth*
> *Even midwinter flowers freeze, I call*
> *The color of cold flesh*
> *I call shrilly in the whirling wind*
> *And walk on alone, just walk on.*
>
> *Like mud at the bottom of a dirty pond*
> *The weakness of this stomach*
> *No one can laugh at it*
> *I throw memories around me like a shawl*
> *And ask why the world is empty*
>
> *Human beings turn to dust*
> *Even my stored-up breath will fade*
> *In the midst of this rise and fall*
> *I sing a song about loving a man*
> *It makes a hellish sound*
> *Joining the noise of rough breathing*
>
> *There's no one to ask*
> *There's no sense in waiting*
> *Beans of this floating world pop open*
> *Glass of this empty earth*
> *Glass of this bright and blooming earth.*

Good or bad, rich or poor, I live silently in the midst of all kinds of echoes, a single amoeba. Mother returned to the country two days ago. I've set my mind to living a better life than I have until now. The thought of dying repells me! I have the human desire to survive, no matter what. A postcard comes from Nomura. He has moved. "Somehow or other I've managed to regain an optimistic way of living." He says to come by for a visit and thanks me for my recent letter; he received the money.

Suddenly, my heart races. I get off the streetcar at Sakana-cho in Ushigome and walk past the post office, turn a corner by a bank and reach a small apartment building, painted red, with a liquor store next door. I'm told that Nomura lives in Apartment 7 on the second floor. I go up and knock. An un-furnished room.

He stands up, wearing a hat as if he is about to go out some-where. I smile, feeling awkward. He grins. When I say how nice his new place is, he answers that he recently published a book of poetry, and that from now on he should be much better off. Even so, the room is empty. Nomura says he is on his way to eat at a café, and he asks to borrow fifty sen. We leave together.

In front of the liquor store lies a drunken old woman in a thin jacket. Through the rope curtain screening the doorway I can see a crowd of people milling about. The shop looks as popular as a public bath.

We walk to Iidabashi and go to a place called the Shōchiku. The tables are dusty. Eating rice with fish and soup, we are like a married couple that has made up after an argument. Even though I know I'll use up my money if I am with this man, I feel cheerful and make a show of answering him agreeably. I forget how miserable I used to be when I lived with him.

Nomura tells me how he has recently been receiving a larger fee for his poetry. The Shinchōsha publishing house paid him six yen for one poem. I am envious. We leave the café and walk back to Ushigome. At the post office, Nomura sees a pudgy man with a heavy beard and greets him politely. He tells me this man, named Suzuki, works for Shinchōsha. Now I understand why he had to greet him deferentially, I think.

I start to feel as lonely as if a temple bell had been struck inside me. What a wretched occupation writing is. By selling one poem a year for six yen, you can't make a living, I say to Nomura. He looks annoyed and spits loudly.

When I say good-bye in front of his apartment building, Nomura doesn't even look at me before going up the stairs. I don't know what to do. I think of the haiku poem, "In the morning mist, the two of us stand in the kitchen." Remembering our life of poverty together at Tamagawa, I pick up my clogs and go up to the second floor. When I open the door, I find Nomura reading, his hat still on his head. I don't know any more if I like this man or hate him. After sitting for a while, I decide to go back to the café. "I'm going to leave now. I'll come again soon." As I speak, Nomura picks up a knife and flings it at me. The small blade sticks in the tatami. I gasp. So he still has this disgusting habit. When we lived at Seta, he threw a knife at me several times. I can't move, knowing that if I stand up, he will grab me by the legs and push me down. Outside I can see the cold sky threatening rain.

Someone knocks at the door. I get up and open it. Standing there is a young man I've never seen before. To me he seems like a god of mercy, and I invite him in, then pick up my clogs and go out into the corridor. Nomura calls to me and follows me out into the hallway, but I hurry out the door. My head hurts as if I am catching the flu.

Walking along a narrow street in Yokoderachō, I think of Yoshitsune of Asakusa. Now I feel grateful for his words: he said he loves me platonically.

When I'm alone, I become a wild woman.

Nighttime.

Just as I begin to drunkenly sing a song for the customers, Nomura comes into the café. I stop singing. It's not my turn to serve the customers, but I know that he has no money. I feel a bitterness in my chest.

Sourly playing a mouth harp, Katsumi brings him sake. My legs feel weak. I call Katsumi to the back room and tell her Nomura knows me and doesn't have any money. She understands and goes back. I leave from the back door just as I am and walk toward the red-light district. Mr. Kan of the *tatami* shop stops me and asks where I am going. Out to buy cigarettes, I say. He offers to treat me to sushi so we go together to a sushi stall. Kan is a good *shinnai* singer. I hear that he keeps a mistress on the second floor of a laundry.

I take my time returning to the café and find that Nomura is still there. He is drinking sake and eating fried rice with a peaceful expression. I think I would sacrifice anything for him. Nomura leaves at about ten p.m.

Feeling that I am about to sink into the ground, I realize that there is no such thing as love.

Original title: *Hōrōki* (1927).

Nakamoto Takako

(1903-   )

A COMMON PROBLEM in recovering women's literary heritage is that many writers' works have been lost. Such is the case with Nakamoto Takako. Most of the novels and short stories she wrote are now inaccessible, since they were not collected in any of the anthologies of modern Japanese fiction published in the past several decades. A thorough study of Takako's work and her contribution to the history of the women writers in modern Japan is yet to be made, and only the barest details of her life are known.

"I was the poorest student, wearing the most shameful clothes," wrote Takako in a brief autobiographical account of her childhood. Her father, a retired army officer and high school gym teacher, had moved his family from a remote village to the city of Yamaguchi so that his children could receive secondary education. It was here that Takako suddenly discovered how poor her family was. Nonetheless, Takako, the eldest child, was able to go to a four-year girls' high school with her father's encouragement. She was a good student, excelling particularly in math and chemistry, and also developed an interest in literature thanks to an innovative teacher. Taking advantage of the large city library, Takako became an avid reader of contemporary Japanese fiction and poetry as well as the classics of world literature. After completing high school, she taught at a primary school, but she felt stifled and restless and thought more and more about going to Tokyo. Like so many ambitious young women of that time, Takako looked to Tokyo as a city of endless opportunity and a place to shape her own future. With a friend who had similar dreams, she arrived there in 1927.

Not much is known about how Takako managed to make a

living in Tokyo, but her goal was clearly to become a writer. While still living in Yamaguchi, Takako had been corresponding with Yokomitsu Riichi, a champion of the Neo-Sensualism school of writing, and through this contact she was able to get a job at one of the leading publishing houses. Though her job consisted mainly of running errands and fetching manuscripts from various authors, she did manage to make some contacts with editors and eventually succeeded in being asked to write stories for a journal called *Creative Writing Monthly* (*Sosaku Gekkan*). She was also introduced to Kikuchi Kan, the legendary publisher and popular fiction writer who was known for his financial support to unknown writers. It is said that he also took advantage of aspiring young women writers by exploiting them sexually. Takako and other young women writers felt frustrated by their dependency on these exclusively male editors, and they were quick to respond to the opportunity to publish their work in *Women and the Arts* (*Nyonin Geijitsu*), the magazine started in 1928 to promote literary women.

While Hayashi Fumiko was perhaps the best-known beneficiary of *Women and the Arts*, there were several other women writers, including Takako, who were greatly encouraged by the opportunity to publish work in this magazine. Mostly young and from various parts of Japan, these women came to Tokyo with the dream of becoming writers. Under the leadership of Hasegawa Shigure, the magazine's publisher and a writer herself, the women provided each other with mutual support for their literary endeavors as well as for their social and political activities. Though the magazine's original stance was politically neutral, it was soon heavily influenced by the leftist school of writing, reflecting the general trend of the times. In the second year of publication the editors began issuing supplements intended to enlighten the less-educated women of the working class. One story published in such a supplement, for example, records the narrator's attempt to escape from a geisha house and free herself from indentured slavery. Some of the women writers were more interested in fiction as a tool of social change rather than a means of artistic expression, and their writing was generally naive and poorly executed. Their works nonetheless vividly expressed their outrage about sexual oppression and exploitation, and successfully conveyed the message that women would no longer be victimized.

In 1929 Takako published her first piece in *Women and the Arts*, a short story entitled "Red" (*Aka*), which describes women toiling in day-to-day physical labor. Only a few months later another of her stories, "The Female Bell-Cricket" (*Suzumushi no Mesu*), appeared in the same magazine. With its deliberately prosaic style and vivid, sometimes strange, sensuous images, the story reflects the principles of modernism introduced in the 1920s by Neo-Sensualists such as Yokomitsu Riichi and Kowobata Yasunari. A powerful narrative of a woman who takes advantage of her weak and idealistic lover, "The Female Bell-Cricket" was the first story written by a Japanese woman that openly depicted a woman's sexual desire. Takako called it "a story of fantasy" yet its theme is a militant expression of a woman's need to control her life. The work received a rave review in the national newspaper, *Asahi*, and overnight Takako had made herself a name in the literary world.

Instead of continuing on with her literary career, however, Takako decided to leave writing for a time so that she could devote herself to organizing workers. She wasn't very pleased with the stories she had written and felt she needed direct contact with working women. In the fall of 1929 she moved to a working-class neighborhood in Tokyo where several large cotton mills were located, including Tōyō Muslin. Takako began her career as an activist by organizing the textile workers of this factory. The workers were mostly young women from rural areas who lived in company dormitories, and in 1927 they had gone on strike and won the right to go out at night—a major victory. A dispute in 1930 protesting the dismissal of a large number of employees, however, ended in a disastrous defeat. Fighting the police and the company "goon squad" with bamboo spears and other make-shift weapons, the young women workers, many of them in their teens, were quickly overwhelmed. Takako was among the two hundred who were arrested at this battle. She spent thirty-one days in prison.

While she was recuperating after her release from prison, Takako was contacted by a member of the Communist Party and asked to become a "sympathizer," a term used for individuals who were not Party members but supported the Party through fundraising, message delivery and, in the case of women, performing domestic chores for male members. Takako agreed and for several months was involved in illegal activities until she was arrested again, this time by the secret service section of the police. She was brutally interrogated and tortured by the police and as a result suffered a severe nervous breakdown and was sent to a mental hospital. After her release from the mental hospital, Takako, still on probation, went to Kawasaki, an industrial city near Tokyo, and worked in a ceramic tile factory. This was in defiance of probation orders, and when she was discovered she was sentenced to three years in prison.

By this time Takako had become deeply committed to the communist cause both in action and in writing. While working at the ceramic tile factory, she wrote a novel based on her experience at Tōyō Muslin and published it under the title *Factory Number Four, the Tōyō Muslin* (*Tō-mosu Daiyon Kōjō*) in *Women and the Arts*. This was her last work to appear in the magazine, which was discontinued in 1936 because of the financial difficulties caused by repeated government orders prohibiting sales of the magazine. (Hasegawa Shigure, the publisher, started another small journal to keep in contact with the women writers. This magazine, *To Glow* (*Kagayaku*), would eventually come to support the government's war effort.) By the early 1930s it was impossible to write anything with a theme even slightly critical of the military regime, and subtle changes began appearing in the fiction of Takako as well as that of other young writers over the next several years.

It is generally believed that Takako recanted her communist beliefs under police pressure, probably at the time of her last arrest. Her story, "Working in Uniform" (*Hakui Sagyo*),

written in 1937 and published in a commercial literary magazine, describes interactions between political prisoners and
other women prisoners without any apparent political message. This piece was notable as the first work of fiction written
by a woman describing the women's prison. Her next two
novels revealed some significant changes in her writing: the
workers in *Nanbu Iron Kettle Makers* (*Nanbu Tetsu-bin Kō*,
1938) no longer engage in strikes but organize themselves in an
effort to increase their productivity. Similarly, *Dark and Bright
Sides of Construction* (*Kensetsu no Meian*, 1939) deals with the
iron workers' involvement in the factory's decision to switch
from manufacturing kettles to contributing to the war industry. This type of fiction was referred to as "Productivity Literature" (*Seisan Bungaku*) and its central concern was to describe
people working in support of their country, which was badly
in need of increased productivity. Many other writers contributed to this body of literature as well, an indication of their
vulnerability under the military state. Takako's novels of this
period, though well researched, are superficial and lack artistic
integrity.

Takako did not write between 1941 and 1952; like most other Japanese writers she was primarily concerned with physical
survival. She married and had two children during this period,
and when the war ended and other women writers such as
Hirabayashi Taiko and Miyamoto Yuriko resumed writing,
she was busy raising a family. Her husband, a Communist
Party member, lost his job in civil service as the result of the
"red purge," a policy of the U.S. Occupational Government,
and her family suffered many financial hardships. Her first
work after the war, "A Tiny Crippled Fly" (*Bikko no Ko-bai*,
1954) is a realistic story about a family put under constant
surveillance by the police, seen through the eyes of a young
child. Takako was productive in the latter half of the 1950s,
and in addition to the novel *Runways* (*Kassōro*), which was
serialized in the *Red Flag* (*Akahata*), a daily paper of the Japanese Communist Party, and translated into Chinese and Russian, she wrote a novel based on her family.

Takako's creative activity continued throughout the 1960s;

she wrote several more novels, including an autobiographical account of her earlier experiences in prisons and the mental hospital. In 1962 she published "My Record of the Anti-Security Treaty Campaign" (*Watashi no Ampo-Tōsō Nikki*), which described her involvement in the nationwide demonstrations against the military treaties between the United States and Japan. During the 1970s Takako was engrossed in the study of Japanese classics, but in 1984 she once again took up her pen, this time to write about the A-bomb victims in Hiroshima. Now in her eighties, Takako remains very active and has remarked that there are many more issues she would like to write about.

Y. T.

The Female Bell-Cricket

translated by Yukiko Tanaka

In a corner of the last streetcar of the day, Tomoko sat, her chin buried deep in the collar of her overcoat. She felt as if her voice were caught in her throat, like a broken musical instrument. The streetcar was nearly empty but the air was filled with the smell of sour alcohol. Each time the train jerked, Tomoko's lackluster hair swayed, disturbing her shadow on the wall. She felt as if the train were hurling her into the depths of the ocean; it was difficult to breathe. Inhaling greedily, her nostrils flaring, Tomoko gazed inquisitively at the passengers.

Men! They are all hefty men! she thought. Moved by this sudden realization of their male sex, she was breathless. For a moment she forgot that her stomach was empty, shrunken like a paper balloon—she had been wandering around all day. The next moment she heard her own voice scolding her for being helplessly attracted to men, even after Akita, her common-law husband, had betrayed and left her.

Tomoko got off the train and started walking briskly, her thin shoulders braced as if the air were assaulting her. Stone buildings stood indifferent and cold, making the street look as narrow as a fjord. The bare branches lining the street sliced the cold air. As she walked along, following her black shadow, Tomoko felt like spitting on herself out of hostility and self-disgust.

The roof on the other side of the bridge was lower, making

the town look much less intimidating. But the pressure of the
wind grew stronger, and Tomoko felt her body being pushed
along. She was already at the outskirts of the city. After the
cold concrete pavement, the resilience and the rich smell of soil
overwhelmed her. At the left side of the road was a huge pile of
dirt, fenced off with a rope. Inside the enclosure, a lantern
illuminated a close-cropped head and a shovel going up and
down in a regular rhythm. Occasionally the tip of the shovel
flashed an icy glitter. Walking on, she felt something cold on
the end of her nose; she stuck out her hand and some chilly
drops of water fell onto her palm. No sooner did she realize
what this was than she was enveloped in rain, which beat
down on the rooftops with increasing force. Blown by the
wind, the rain pelted against the ground with the strength of
horses' hooves. The driving rain spashed in Tomoko's face as
she stood in the middle of the road. She pulled up the collar of
her coat and hurried on, her body bent so low that she was
almost crawling under the eaves of the houses. The rain trick-
led through her collar and down her back. The sole reason for
her being out late on a night like this was the same as for all the
other nights: to indulge in sex with Akita before he took his
new bride, to feel superior to the bride-to-be. Akita's parents
had refused to recognize Tomoko as their son's common-law
wife.

   The house she was returning to stood in front of her, shabby
as a small paper box, desolate and trembling in the gusty wind.
The first thing that Tomoko sensed as her shivering hand
pulled the door open was the smell of a male body. She was
once again overcome by self-disgust as she remembered how
she had reacted earlier to the odor of men in the streetcar. She
went in, noisily. Under the dim light of the lamp, Miki sat
hunched over his desk. This man, poor and gentle as a doe,
had rescued Tomoko and was providing her with shelter and
food. She stood in front of him and stared coldly at his pale
forehead, half-covered by hair. She directed her pent-up anger
at him, ready to explode.

   "Look, I'm drenched," she said, shaking herself hard and
pulling at the sleeve of her coat. She looked around the room.

Finding no charcoal left in the brazier and therefore no fire with which to dry herself, she went to the closet and yanked a dress out of her wicker trunk. Seeing Tomoko's anger, Miki looked at her apologetically.

"You must be cold. I'm sorry I don't have a fire," he said.

Without responding, Tomoko took off her wet clothes in front of him and dried herself with a towel. When her body had regained its warmth and color, she put on dry clothes. The wind outside had begun to blow harder against the houses and the ground.

Sullenly she went to the kitchen to find something to eat. In a pot was a bit of cold rice, gleaming faintly in the light. There was also some salted seaweed in a sake cup.

"Have you eaten?" she asked Miki, glancing at the food.

"Yes, I have," he said firmly. But she knew that he hadn't. The rice in the pan was the same as it had been when she left the house. Realizing that Miki had saved the food for her even though he was hungry himself, she was filled with an even stronger contempt for him. She felt no gratitude for his kindness and gentleness. She knew where his ambition lay, she could see it more clearly everyday. Men are all kind and gentle until they get what they want from a woman, she thought. She went ahead and ate the food as if she were entitled to it.

Tomoko's body, which had been chilled to the bone, now felt warmer. After she had eaten what little food there was, she began spreading the quilts out next to Miki, who was still sitting at the desk. On the desert of the sheet Tomoko found a pubic hair. I shall let this lie modestly in a piece of tissue paper, she thought, and held it in her palm to inspect it under the light. She sighed deep and long, a sigh long as a comet's tail.

Tomoko grew plump as the days went by and her skin became silky. Miki, on the other hand, became pale and skinny. He had only a few books left; his violin had been exchanged long ago for rice and charcoal. His cloak had flown away like a butterfly, transformed into a piece of steak, into hot chicken with rice, into colorful salads. The only regular income Miki had was from writing a few pages of poetry, which he sold for ten yen to a stationery outfit in Kanda. The poems adorned the covers of stationery, intended to inspire the hearts of naive teenage girls. The money earned was quickly changed into meat and vegetables; the only trace of his labors was the faint smell of fat at the bottom of a cooking pan. Miki also worked long hours as a copyist, but even so he could not keep up with Tomoko's appetite. Still, he was pleased that Tomoko had stopped chasing after Akita and was no longer going out so often, instead spending most of her time lying beside him.

Tomoko felt dried up, like a scab on an old wound. She had no desire to work; respectable jobs all seemed absurd, and any effort of a philosophical nature she considered useless. Look at the way people live in this large city, she thought: they flourish like cryptogamous plants; they conceal strange bacteria as they live day to day. She spent her days observing the man gasping beside her, indifferent to what she saw; she could have been watching a plastic doll. Sometimes she stared at his fine Roman nose, thinking that she would some day kill this man and eat him, just as the female bell-cricket devours her mate.

Tomoko sat on the sunny windowsill, her clothes slipped down to her waist. She was hunting for fleas in her underwear. The fleas, which had been hiding inside the seams, jumped in small, perfect arcs on the faded pink fabric. She pursued them with concentration. Miki watched, enjoying the curves of Tomoko's body—from her forehead to her nose, then to her chin, from her neck down to her breasts. When his eyes reached her two shiny cones, he quickly averted them, blinking; he felt his cigarette burning his fingertips and threw it away. He returned his gaze to Tomoko, but by this time the cones were hidden behind her arms, the wonderful opportunity to enjoy her was lost. His face revealed his desire to lie in her arms and suck at her breast, as he had at his mother's. But this was a fantasy, he knew, and he forced himself to go back to his book.

After she had killed all the fleas she could find, Tomoko slipped her soft body back into her clothes and spanned her waist with her hands to measure it. Then she went over to

Miki and, squatting down by his desk, moved her knees back and forth like a pet dog wagging its tail.

"I feel like eating a steak tonight," she said.

"Tonight?" Miki said nervously. "But we had chicken cutlets last night, so . . ."

"That was yesterday."

"But . ." The man still hesitated. Tomoko kept staring at him as he turned his face away.

"But there's no money. Is that what you're saying? There are many ways to get money."

Miki bit his lip and lowered his head, supporting it in his hands and staring at the vacant space in front of him. He saw before him the shadow of this woman whose body had filled out and whose skin was now lustrous. Tomoko was aware of her power over Miki, who sat silently. She watched him indifferently, smoking her cigarette.

"You haven't got your pay from that place in Kanda, have you?"

"I got it for the work I did this month. And the day before yesterday I took in the work I was supposed to do for next month," he said, slowly opening his eyes. His voice was low and sad, like the sound a cat makes when it's been smacked on the forehead.

"How about asking to get paid for that work? You have to be a bit aggressive about these things."

"I see."

"This is what I don't like," she said, shaking her head. Her face was tense, her muscles tight. "Men are attractive when they're pushy and tough. Being timid and reserved like you doesn't impress anyone."

She exhaled as she lifted her chin. The smoke came out of her tilted nose and floated upward. She felt pleased with herself.

"And your poems—they are no good. So old-fashioned. They're sentimental, too. You ought to change your approach altogether."

"I'll go to Kanda, then, even though I don't think I can get any more money," said Miki, who had been listening to To-

moko with his chin resting on his hand. He shook his thin
shoulders. Tomoko sat puffing smoke rings while he went out
the door.

When Miki came back that evening, he handed her, with a
deep sigh, a mere one yen bill. He must have begged it from
the stationery store. Saying he had a stomach ache, he let Tomoko eat the whole steak, shining with fat. The thick, warm
steak titillated Miki's nose with its wonderful smell, while
satisfying juices fell on Tomoko's tongue. She enjoyed every
bite while she watched Miki clutching his stomach, which she
knew was growling from hunger. Does he feel heroic and self-
satisfied? she wondered. If so I'll kick him in the back.

The next day Tomoko found the announcement of Akita's
wedding in the newspaper, accompanied by a photograph. He
had transformed himself back into the son of a comfortable
middle-class family. How painlessly he had taken a lovely
maiden for his wife. In the photograph the bride and groom
looked like a pair of butterflies, like insect specimens. Tomoko
wanted to spit on the picture and throw it at Miki. Instead, she
cut it out and pinned it on the wall. She decided to congratulate
the pair of butterflies with rowdy laughter, but soon her
laughter turned to crying, the tears dripping down and making dark spots on her knees.

Miki watched without a word from where he sat on the
windowsill, cleaning his ears. It was a nice day and Tomoko
invited him to take a walk to an open field nearby. They sat
with their legs stretched out on the withered grass. The late
November sun cast soft, transparent rays on their backs. Tomoko's lavishly padded hips overshadowed Miki's pencil-thin
body. He sat quietly with his eyes half closed, basking in the
sun and the pressure of her body and female odor, and tried to
conjure up some poetic sentiment to suit his mood.

As the days passed, Tomoko grew fatter; she sprawled im-
modestly in front of the man. She had a double chin now, and
her hips were as full and solid as the body of a female moth.
Miki grew thinner; his bones showed beneath his skin. Exhaling black breath from his rancid lungs and suffering from ane-
mic dizziness, he would not give up his woman, whose splen-

did energy and strength was a pleasure to his eyes.

And indeed Tomoko's body was deserving of admiration. Her supple skin was as smooth and shiny as rare Occidental parchment, and in the darkness he was sure he could see a halo around her body. When the small crimson lips above her chin—as full as those of an image of Buddha—were open, her small, well-shaped white teeth gleamed. Her inner thighs were as taut as newly strung rackets, revealing their marvelous flexibility, and when she leaned back in a certain way, her private parts glistened. Living with this glorious female finally led Miki to idolize and worship her. Tomoko only despised him even more, laughing at his hopeless romanticism. She coldly watched as this male bell-cricket became emaciated with the approach of autumn, ready to be eaten by his female.

It became impossible to get money in any way. The copy work done by this man with rancid lungs no longer provided food to satisfy the woman's glorious body. Tossing his pen away, Miki rolled on the floor with his legs and arms pulled up to his chest. Tomoko simply watched him, puffing on her cigarette as she sat on the windowsill.

"What's the matter? You're lazy," she said.

"I can't do it. I'll never catch up," he moaned, gasping his bad breath.

"You're a coward," said Tomoko, and left the window. She went to the mirror to make up her face. Then she changed her clothes and left the house. The man lay on the floor, holding his arms and legs against his abdomen, until she returned late that night.

Tomoko glanced at Miki and sat down next to him on the floor, exposing her nicely shaped legs. Then she took a five-yen bill from her pocket and threw it at him. He got up, about to take the money, and stopped himself. He frowned and stared at the bill for a moment, his eyes filled with doubt. Having reached a conclusion, he stood up, went to the window and took a deep breath. The clear air outside stung him with the sharpness of a neeedle. Looking from the man to the money a few times, Tomoko began to laugh loudly so that her shoulders shook. Her laughter sounded empty, like bones being shaken in a canister.

"You are a fool," she said.

Miki turned around. His unshaven face grew paler. He tried to say something, but no sound came from his distorted mouth. The fact that some physical exercises she had performed earlier that evening had been transformed into a five-yen bill was of no significance to Tomoko. She despised all things that belonged to the abstract arena anyway; she hunted them down like fleas. She had simply thrown her glorious body at a man, a pug-nosed bourgeois, who'd had his eyes on her for some time. That's how she had gotten the money. Ever since losing Akita to another woman, Tomoko felt like a movie screen: after the film of her metaphysical life was finished, the screen reflected only an empty reality. No matter who tried to project an image on the screen, no matter who tried to stir up a physical sensation, the screen remained blank, empty. She picked up the money, looked at it, and started laughing again, loudly.

"What are you thinking, you fool?" She snapped the paper money with her fingers, enjoying its sound, and put it back in her pocket. Then she turned her smile to Miki, who was rubbing his face in confusion. He closed the window and lay down on the floor again. Tomoko lay down next to him.

Tomoko reflected over her current state, comparing it to a few hours earlier, when she had still had a foot in the metaphysical arena. Tomoko discovered that she had neither sadness nor regret. She was now living in a place free of complex thoughts and emotion—and it was far easier. She could blot out her obsessive attachment to Akita and her bitterness toward the city that had engulfed and altered him. But she also felt an even stronger revulsion toward Miki's romanticism, his amiable and timid personality. If he blamed her for what she had done and loved her less because of it, she would grab him like a wild bear, tear his throat with her sharp claws and spill his warm blood.

Moving closer to Miki, Tomoko cornered him; slowly he was backed against the wall. Then she reached out to grab his face and pull it toward her. He looked up with tearful eyes, then suddenly pushed her away, shaking his head fiercely. As she fell backward, he saw her uncovered breast, her arched neck, and the shining hair under her armpits. But even the sight of this did not make Miki want to touch her. Tomoko, who liked being handled roughly, waited in vain for him to grab her. She looked at this man who had turned his back on her, then got up and left the room.

There was a thick fog outside, falling like heavy, milk-colored breath, settling on the ground as it fell. The bare branches of the trees, stretching out like a nervous system, were quickly being covered. Tomoko walked, feeling drops of water form on her eyelids. Night was for those who want to believe in mystery and superstition, she thought. She walked for some time with her hands in her pockets, taking a deep breath once in a while, and then she went back to the house. She went to bed without a word.

With the one yen Tomoko had given him, Miki left the house early in the morning. A day without him seemed emptier than mere physical hunger. She was in anguish all day long; she leaned against the desk and felt like a morning glory in evening. That night she left the door unlocked and waited for him. The clock struck three, then came the first crowing of a cock, but Miki did not return. Toward dawn she fell asleep, still leaning against the desk. When she awakened, Miki was there, the bright morning sunlight on his back.

He stood with the veins showing through the pale skin of his face, his hair mussed. His eyes were wide open. He must have been watching me while I slept, Tomoko thought. His clenched hands shook. Tomoko felt revulsion and anger, but this soon turned to pity and contempt. She couldn't tell whether he had been walking the streets all night or if he'd gone somewhere to buy a prostitute. Either way, she felt he deserved her scorn. He looked at her in confusion, and this made her feel tense; she stared back at him. Unable to bear her gaze, he threw himself to the floor, folded his arms over his chest, and sighed like a person in great distress. His sigh then

turned into painful sobbing. Pretending that she didn't understand, Tomoko continued to stare at him reproachfully. She lit
a cigarette and smoked it slowly, her chin cupped on her hand,
all the while staring at him. When he moved, his kimono fell
open, and she spotted what looked like dried semen on his
thigh. From his body came the rank odor of rotten flesh.

"Why don't you go to the bathhouse today. You haven't
washed in weeks. You ought to clean yourself up," she said,
exhaling smoke toward him.

His eyes closed, Miki lay still for a while, and then, suddenly, he moved, gripping his throat. Gasping hard, as if something were forcing its way from his chest, he covered his
mouth with a handkerchief. When he took it away from his
mouth, he saw a clot of blood, dark red, staring up at his
darkened eyes. He folded the handkerchief and feebly threw
his head down against his outstretched arms. Tomoko sat by
this man, still smoking, watching him coolly.

Original title: *Suzumushi no Mesu* (1929).

Nogami Yaeko

(1885–1985)

IN THE SUMMER OF 1984, a big party was held in Tokyo to celebrate the one-hundredth birthday of Nogami Yaeko. Among the people attending were many major figures from the Japanese literary world. Shortly afterward, her autobiographical novel, *The Wood* (*Mori*), not yet completed, Yaeko died. She had been working on the novel for over ten years by then, at a pace that suited her—slowly and steadily. Yaeko's disciplined approach to her writing, sustained even while in her nineties, was the hallmark of her work. Her remarkably long and productive career spanned eight decades—her first published story appeared in 1911. Though she had neither a brilliant debut like that of her friend Miyamoto Yuriko, nor the financial success achieved by Hayashi Fumiko, Yaeko's accomplishments as a writer were equally impressive. Her critical mind and rigorous self-discipline helped her write fiction with a perspective far beyond her limited personal experiences, and she established an independence few other women writers of her time were able to achieve. Several of her novels stand today as masterpieces of modern Japanese fiction.

Yaeko was born a decade earlier than most of the other women writers represented in this anthology, and she grew up in the more liberal socio-cultural milieu that existed prior to the nationalistic backlash of the 1910s. The eldest daughter of a prosperous sake-manufacturing family, she was born in a small port town of a southern island, Kyūshū. Her father was a liberal-minded man who had inherited his growing business from his own father; her mother was a quiet, loving woman. The people of Yaeko's hometown were unusually progressive for the generally conservative region of Kyūshū, perhaps because the seaport allowed them access to the larger world. One of Yaeko's uncles, for example, studied in the United States and received a graduate degree in economics there. Yaeko's parents did not think it unusual to send their daughter off to Tokyo for her secondary education. By the time Yaeko was ready for this journey, she had already developed a rigorous routine that included private lessons early in the morning, before she left for school. An exceptionally studious girl, Yaeko learned most of the Japanese and Chinese classics in her early teens. Her love of learning and her disciplined determination, nourished at an early age, never diminished.

Yaeko attended the Meiji School for Girls from the time she turned fifteen until she was twenty-two, and there she had many direct and indirect contacts with the pioneers dedicated to the work of modernizing Japan. This was a time when women's emancipation had emerged as an important social issue, and the Meiji School for Girls was an institution with uniquely feminist ideals. It was run by a Christian man who firmly believed that education should transcend nationalistic ideology and that men and women were equal before God. Many years later, Yaeko remarked that she had spent her seven years at the Meiji School for Girls without ever learning the Educational Rescript, the government's official guideline of education, which was based on nationalistic ideology and forced on students at nearly every school. Instead she had the good fortune, during her most impressionable years, of learning to think freely, distrust conventions, and resist authority. She also received basic training in the appreciation of Western literature, philosophy and aesthetics, which were taught by teachers who were themselves writers and critics. During Yaeko's last year, the Meiji School for Girls was closed, largely because of the prevailing anti-Christian mood which had by then settled over the country. In its place, the Japan Women's College was established, an institution that adopted a more reactionary approach to educating women based on the "good wife and wise mother" doctrine.

Compared to many women writers who were her contemporaries, Yaeko led a relatively uneventful and sheltered life. As soon as she finished secondary school in 1906, she married

Nogami Toyoichirō, a young man from her native town, also in Tokyo to study. It is very likely that Yaeko decided to marry Toyoichirō so she could remain in Tokyo and live her life the way she wanted. She could not have hoped for a more accommodating and understanding husband. As Yaeko established her writing career, Toyoichirō carried out all of her necessary and mundane tasks, from dealings with the publishers to buying stamps.

It was through Toyoichirō that Yaeko's work first came to the attention of the professor-turned novelist Natsume Sōseki, one of the most important writers of modern Japanese fiction. Toyoichirō, interested in writing himself, was a regular member of Sōseki's literary salon. He brought Yaeko's stories to Sōseki, who read them and wrote detailed comments. A scholar of English literature, Sōseki recommended that Yaeko read Jane Austen, the Brönte sisters and George Eliot. He also introduced her to theories of literary realism, which encouraged her to write about the details of everyday life. Though Yaeko never attended the salon herself, partly out of shyness, she benefited a good deal from her mentor's indirect teaching and support, and by the time her second child was born, she had published several short stories.

Yaeko's situation was remarkable in that she was able to successfully combine raising a family with establishing her writing career. She was fortunate to have the help of a supportive husband and maids, a luxury enjoyed by few women writers, and she was very conscious of her need for a stable, orderly environment. She did not long to be a public figure, or a member of literary circles, but seemed to prefer the quiet privacy of her home. Yaeko described her approach to her work as that of an "amateur," suggesting that writing was a way to grow into a better and wiser person, not a stepping stone to fame. Always the diligent student, Yaeko worked hard to develop her writing skills and expand her artistic horizons. She read widely in literature as well as in philosophy and history, and took lessons in the tea ceremony and *utai*, the songs accompanying the Noh play. Even during World War II, when her family fled into a remote mountainous region, she

managed to continue her lessons with a prominent philoso-
pher, who had also fled Tokyo.

Yaeko was a prolific writer, publishing over 150 titles in
many different genre: plays, prose fiction, essays, reviews,
biographies, travel accounts and a number of pieces for children. She also worked as a translator, publishing one book of
translation from English every year, a task she imposed on
herself in the early stages of her career so her English wouldn't
become rusty. It is interesting to note that her first attempt at
translation was the biography of the Polish mathematician
Sonya Kovalevsky, a woman she admired for her desire to
learn and her ability to maintain independence within her mar-
rige. Several of Yaeko's pieces were published in the feminist
magazine *Seitō*, and while she was not directly involved in the
publication of the magazine, her contribution to it was significant.

Yaeko's literary themes were as wide-ranging as her personal interests. She was the first modern Japanese author to write
stories from the perspective of a mother of young children. In
A New Life (*Atarashiki Inochi*), a collection of stories published
in 1916, Yaeko portrayed children through the eyes of young
mothers, using this point of view to critically view society.
This innovation was very effective and demonstrated Yaeko's
increasing skill as a fiction writer. She moved on to new
themes in *The Neptune* (*Kaijinmaru*, 1922). Based on an actual
event, this novella about a shipwreck and the ensuing canni-
balism is a vividly gruesome human drama that poses profound questions about human nature. This work helped to
silence critics who claimed that women were incapable of
writing about events and themes outside the confines of their
everyday existence. Yaeko surprised the literary establishment
again a few years later with the publication of *Ōishi Yoshio*, a
novel about an immensely popular historical figure of the
eighteenth century. In her treatment, she challenged the accepted public image of this national hero by depicting him as a
man unsure of himself, trapped by the events of history.

In 1928 Yaeko wrote *Machiko*, a novel based on her observations of the decade's political upheavals, especially their effect

on young people. Machiko, the heroine of the novel, is a bright and sensitive young woman studying sociology. Concerned with her social responsibility, Machiko rejects her family's bourgeois conventions and sympathizes with leftist activists. She eventually comes to see, however, the hyposcrisy in her leftist lover and his excuse that theory and practice are not the same. At the heart of the novel is the dilemma between rationality and passion, both of which were equally authentic to Yaeko.

Politics and power interested Yaeko greatly. Over a period extending from 1937 to 1956, Yaeko wrote *The Labyrinth* (*Meiro*), a novel in five volumes. It is an ambitious work that examines many layers of Japanese society—the upper-class politicians and businessmen, the working-class revolutionaries, the traditional artists and scholars. Seen through the eyes of a young man who has renounced his leftist beliefs, the novel portrays a civilization on the brink of self-destruction. *The Labyrinth* has a complex and a symphonic structure unparalleled by the work of any woman writer in modern Japanese literature.

Yaeko's recurring theme—and her own personal conviction—was that among all human endeavors, only art transcends time. She took up this idea once again in her historical novel *Hideyoshi and Rikyū*, published in 1962 and for which she received a prestigious literary prize. The novel deals with a conflict between Rikyu, a famous sixteenth-century artist and tea master, and Hideyoshi, a political genius who ruled Japan. By the time Yaeko wrote this novel she had been writing for over half a century.

Besides the many years it spanned and the wide range of topics addressed, what is striking about Yaeko's career is the continual development of her work—from short, often sketchy stories to full-length, complex novels of almost perfect form. Unlike many other women writers of her time, she did not write autobiographical fiction until the very end of her career. In a literary climate in which the confessional form was favored, critical evaluation of Yaeko's fiction was not always positive; in fact, her work has rarely been given the credit it deserves. It was not until 1964, when she was nearly eighty years old, that Yaeko was awarded the Women's Literary Prize, and even then she did not enjoy much acclaim. This tempered response, however, might have been what she preferred.

Y. T.

A Story of a Missing Leg

translated by Yukiko Tanaka

I received a letter one day from a woman who was a total stranger to me. She said in the letter that her eighteen-year-old niece, who had lost one arm in an accident when she was a child, was very fond of reading, and that, though it was only a layman's view, she appeared to have some talent in writing. She had thought that it would be wonderful if her niece could try to establish herself as a writer. She wanted to tell me more about the girl, to know what I thought of her idea. Could I spare some time to see her?

Writers who are better known than I am probably receive letters like this quite often, but unfortunately, or fortunately, I rarely have the pleasure of receiving such requests. Looking at the faltering style of the characters written on the card—it was one of those double cards, half of which can be used for the reply—I saw that the sender barely managed to say what she wanted. I had a hard time forming an image of the woman, whose name was Takayama Mine. Judging from her handwriting she could not have gone to school beyond sixth grade. Her address was Futabacho, in Honjo. A woman who lived in Honjo, and who wrote this letter, had an idea of making her crippled niece into a writer. This fact made me curious. I was further intrigued by the fact that she had chosen me, not a popular writer, but one whose writing tends to be overly serious. So I felt like breaking my rule this time—I usually refuse to meet with strangers—and decided to go ahead and see her. Using the simplest words possible, I wrote on the reply card that it was extremely difficult to support oneself as a writer but if she still wanted to talk to me she could come to see me on any day that suited her.

The woman came several days later. It was early in the morning, and since I had forgotten who she was, I had to send the maid back to find out the nature of the visit. The maid came back with the reply card I had sent.

"Oh, yes, the woman from Honjo." I was in the middle of fixing my hair just then and told the maid to have her wait upstairs. While she was preparing the tea, I asked if the visitor was alone. When it turned out that she was, I felt a slight disappointment, and then a twinge of guilt. I was obviously curious about her crippled niece and wanted to see the girl— even though I had so completely forgotten about the letter that the woman's name had not rung a bell. I went upstairs, where I found a fair, plump middle-aged woman, reserved in manner, sitting in a corner of the room, having declined to use the floor cushion offered to her. With her old-fashioned hairdo, she looked like a typical working-class housewife.

"Please, come and sit here, don't put yourself in a corner like that," I said, urging her to sit across from me at the table. She did so, and started telling me about her niece. The girl, she said, was actually the niece of her husband, and lived with her parents in the country. I was somewhat surprised to hear this as I had supposed that the girl was living with her.

"Where exactly is her home?"

"It's in the Echigo area, up from Kashiwazaki; quite a ways up the mountain, ma'am, yes indeed."

Twelve or thirteen years ago, the woman went on, a reservoir had been built near the girl's home. The workers used a handcar to haul the dirt away from the construction site. It was the largest undertaking of its kind in the village and a rare occasion for the children. They were fascinated by the handcar that ran as if by magic on two iron strips—so fast and smooth! Naturally they couldn't resist trying it for themselves and they asked to play on it whenever it wasn't being used by the construction crew. The handcar became the favorite toy for the village children, and no one listened when the teacher cautioned them that it was dangerous. It was this handcar that took the arm of the woman's niece.

"She was five then, and her grandmother was watching after her. But it was the handcar, you know, and it all happened in the twinkling of an eye. The old grandmother is still alive, she's seventy-three this year. She's been saying ever since the accident that it was her fault for letting it happen when the child was in her care. She says she'll carry her regret beyond the grave unless the girl's future is settled—a way she can support herself, you know," the woman said in a crisp voice.

I also learned that the girl had lost her mother shortly after her birth, that she'd had three stepmothers, and that she had taken care of her brothers and sisters by all these different mothers despite her physical handicap. The woman also related that the girl was very good at sewing. She could even use the sewing machine, though no one knew how she managed to do it. More than anything else, however, she liked reading and writing. Her letters telling about her situation at home and expressing her sadness, were so well written that the aunt wept in sympathy when she read them.

"So, since she can't get married like normal girls, and she has to find a way to support herself, I thought she should try what she really likes to do," the woman concluded.

Supporting oneself by doing what one really likes to do. What a wonderful way to live, and how difficult it is, I thought to myself. It's rare in this society to be able to make a living by doing what we truly love, particularly if you are an artist. So I asked the woman what kind of education the girl had.

"She's finished grammar school in the village."

"What kinds of books does she like to read, then?"

"Well, her folks are farmers from deep in the mountains, so she can't be choosy. I send her the magazines I subscribe to, *Women's Life* and *Women's World*—things like that. They tell me she reads those day in and day out. She sends me a thank you note each time, and no one can tell, reading them, that they were written by a girl with only one arm."

"And she herself wants to become a writer?"

"Well, that's not exactly it. To tell the truth, it's my idea more or less . . ."

"Excuse me for asking this, but do you and your husband have a business of some kind?"

"Yes, we have, a tinplate shop. We make cans."

The woman then told her own story. She had been married to her present husband for only two years. He had lost his first wife in the Great Earthquake when she and their two older children were stranded at work in a clothing factory demolished in the quake. He was left with the youngest child.

"That's why my husband is easily moved to tears these days and says he wants to do whatever's possible for his niece. I'm ashamed, but to tell the truth, my husband can't read. But his niece writes so well in her letters, and so he is amazed, you see. Myself, I'd rather buy a magazine than go to a movie. I've heard, you know, that writers like you can make a lot of money these days by writing something simple."

A strange feeling of shame overtook me for a moment when the woman said this. At the same time I couldn't help smiling. This last admiring comment made me envision the scene of a wife-and-husband discussion session in the back of a tinplate shop in Honjo: a good-natured husband who is quite skillful with his hands but blind as far as letters goes, a man who has become more apprehensive since the Great Earthquake, and his second wife, whom he probably pampers a little, a woman who likes to read magazines. They must have talked about it over and over again—what to do about the future of their poor crippled niece? And the conclusion they reached was not sewing, not even with a sewing machine, but writing. Times had changed—who would have imagined five years ago that a tinplate shop owner in Honjo and his wife would come up with the idea of training their niece to become a writer, just as they might think of apprenticing their son to some trade or sending their daughter to become a hair stylist.

My response to the woman was merely a recitation of what I had written in my reply. As it always has been, art is the most uncertain, the most risky area in which to try to make a living,

particularly when the aspirant's talent is unknown and she is
not motivated by her own strong desire. It is something that
one cannot recommend for others. Furthermore, if one can
successfully market writing which is not the result of considerable hard work, the work itself is not at all authentic. Listening to her story, I told the woman, made me think that the best
thing she could do would be to encourage her niece to enjoy
more and better reading so that her talent, if she truly had one,
would naturally sprout and grow. I wanted to add, actually,
that I felt sorry for the girl if *Women's Life* and *Women's World*
were all she had to read, but I restrained myself. The woman
seemed to understand without my saying anything more that I
was discouraging her idea. She said she would convey my
suggestion to her husband. She then drank the tea, now cold,
and stood up to leave. Feeling sorry that she was leaving disappointed, I got the idea of giving her some of my old magazines. Pulling several from the stack in the corner of the hallway, I handed them to her to send to her niece.

"All these? Really? Thank you so much."

"Any time, if old ones will do."

"Thank you, these will keep her busy for a long time. I'm
sure she'll be very pleased."

The woman took a wrapping cloth out of her small bag and
wrapped the magazines in it. The only thing left for her to do
was to say goodbye and leave. Instead of doing so, she stood
there, hesitating. Was there anything else she wanted to tell
me? I wondered. I waited for her to begin, watching the uneasy expression on her face. She seemed to be encouraged by
my silent urging and said, "I'm afraid you might be offended,
but to tell the truth, I thought you didn't have a normal body
till I saw you."

This strange confession startled me. What was she trying to
say? Seeing my puzzled look, the woman continued.

"Sometime ago I read in *Housewife's Friend*, I think it was,
some biographies of women writers. It said that even though
you'd lost a leg because of some illness, you became successful. And then there was that example of Tsumakichi, who has
no arms. So I thought, there are people like my niece. I said to

myself that a person like you would be more sympathetic toward her. And now, when I see you, you don't seem to be
missing a leg. . ."

I started to laugh, and the woman laughed also, looking
relieved. I realized right away that she had mistaken me for
that beautiful, tragic, woman writer who walks with crutches.
I understood now why she had come to see me. I had to admire
her cleverness for having chosen a handicapped writer to consult with about her crippled niece. And I had to sympathize
with her astonishment when she saw me, a person who supposedly had only one leg, walk up the stairs and into the room.

"Well, I'd be happy to do anything I can," I said wholeheartedly, wanting to console her. She thanked me, but I sus-
pected that nothing could make up for the leg that wasn't
missing. I watched her walk away, and as she passed through
the gate and under an oleander bush, she seemed despondent.
But perhaps that was just my imagination.

Original title: *Kata-ashi no Mondai* (1931).

Sata Ineko

(1904-)

SATA INEKO CAME INTO THIS WORLD as the result of a youthful romance between an eighteen-year-old boy, the son of a physician and hospital director, and his girlfriend, the fifteen-year-old daughter of a small city postmaster in southern Japan. Ineko was reared by her paternal grandmother after her mother died when she was six years old. Unable to hold a steady job, her father moved frequently, and when the family went to Tokyo, Ineko and her grandmother were forced to go out to work, earning whatever small income they could. When Ineko was eleven years old, an age when most girls were still in primary school, she began working in factories and restaurants. She was never to return to school. Her formal education, terminated before she had completed the fifth grade, was probably the shortest of any major Japanese writer during this century. As a child, however, she went to the public library whenever she had spare time and read, mostly fiction. She had an uncle, a university student and aspiring writer, who supported and encouraged Ineko's interest in literature. By age fourteen, she was reading the works of Shakespeare and Victor Hugo in translation and submitting short stories and poems to *Girls' Friends (Shōjo no Tomo)* and other magazines for teenage girls. Her uncle, the hope of the family and her only mentor, died of consumption before completing his university education, when Ineko was fifteen.

Wrapping caramels and packing them into boxes was the first job Ineko's father found for her the year they went to Tokyo. Ineko, among the youngest of the girls working at the factory, was barely making enough to pay her streetcar fare. When her father realized it didn't make sense for Ineko to commute to the factory, he let her quit. Her next job was at a restaurant, but because she couldn't peel potatoes fast enough, she was fired. She then went to work as a nanny and maid for a family who ran a large restaurant. Ineko was not alone, of course, in working long hours for extremely low wages. World War I brought rapid industrial expansion to Japan, and along with it, high inflation and many labor disputes. The price of rice jumped four times during the summer of 1918, causing the widespread rioting generally referred to as "the rice riots"; these were actually started by housewives in a northeastern fishing village. The factories, particularly in the textile industries, had been hiring many teenage girls (as well as older women) since the 1890s, and by the end of this century's first decade the atrocious working conditions endured by the young women factory workers became a major issue for leftist and humanitarian leaders and sparked the Japanese labor union movement. It was in this turbulent atmosphere that young Ineko spent her days at the factories.

When she saw how hard it was for her grandmother, now working beside her in a knit underwear factory, Ineko wrote to her father, who had by then left Tokyo, and offered to sell herself to a geisha house. Her father instead summoned her to live with him and his second wife in a remote city. Ineko stayed there two years and spent most of her time alone, reading books whenever she could find them and roaming around the neighborhood. In 1919 she returned to Tokyo where she eventually found a job as a department store clerk; although it was more pleasant than working in restaurants, Ineko found the work stifling and monotonous. The store carried mainly imported merchandise, including books, and the customers were either intellectuals, who came to buy the books, or upper-class people, who could afford imported luxuries. Ineko, at age eighteen, was a quiet-mannered young woman and exceptionally pretty. She started writing poetry and became a member of the group writing for a coterie magazine called *Poetry and Life* (*Shi to Jinsei*).

Like many women of her time, marriage appeared to Ineko as the only escape from the monotony of work. When a young man from a well-to-do family asked her, through the manager of the store, to be his wife, she accepted. The marriage lasted for two years. Her husband was an abusive man with complicated family and financial problems. As a result of her despair over this relationship, Ineko attempted suicide twice, failing both times. When she was taken to her father's house after the second attempt, she refused to go back to her husband. At age twenty-two Ineko once again found herself working at a café, but this time with a child to support.

Among the patrons of the café were the poet Nakano Shigeharu and the writer Kubokawa Tsurujirō. When Ineko met them they, along with several other leftist school poets and writers, were starting a literary magazine called *Donkey* (*Roba*). These aspiring young writers and revolutionaries were quite eager to encourage a working woman like Ineko to write; they believed that common people had important things to say and therefore should be helped to express themselves through writing. They also urged Ineko to study Marxist theory. Within a few months she married Kubokawa and by 1929 she was a member of the Communist Writers Federation, having published short stories in such magazines as *The Proletariat Art* (*Puroretaria Geijutsu*) and *A Battle Flag* (*Senki*).

Ineko also succeeded in publishing her work in commercial literary magazines. Her first published story, "From a Caramel Factory" (*Kyarameru Kōjō kara*), is based on Ineko's first job in Tokyo—wrapping and boxing caramels—and her bitter disappointment at having to quit school. While the humiliating experience of young factory workers are convincingly described, the story does not make any overt political statement. It conveys not only the sadness and fear of the girl protagonist toward the unknown world of adults—including her father—but also the tension between victim and victimizer.

For the next several decades, Ineko continued to write fiction based on her own experiences as a woman, wife, mother and committed socialist. She met Miyamoto Yuriko in the year Yuriko returned from Soviet Russia, and they formed a close friendship which lasted till Yuriko's death. Ineko's Communist friends, her husband included, professed to believe that women were independent individuals, not to be subjugated by men, and that they contributed equally to society through their work. This idea was particularly inspiring and encouraging to Ineko. She viewed her participation in socialist activities as an integral part of her activity as a writer. Ineko lived in a working-class neighborhood and became involved in the labor disputes of the textile industry. In 1931, she published a work about the strike at Tōyō Muslin; that same year she became the editor of *Working Women* (*Hataraku Fujin*), a Communist Party publication.

During the 1930s, police suppression of activities critical of the government ultimately silenced most of the Japanese writers unwilling to support the growing military campaign. In 1932, Ineko's husband Kubokawa was taken into the prison, where he stayed for a year. Ineko, who joined the Communist Party in 1932, was also detained for two months. Ineko's sole source of income for herself and her children came from her writing, and the imposed silence was particularly difficult for her. The situation was different for her friend Miyamoto Yuriko, who remained loyal to the Communist Party throughout: childless and with some financial support from her parents, Yuriko could afford to stop writing. But for Ineko, not writing meant not feeding her children. Feeling she could not do otherwise, Ineko continued to publish fiction. Her stories were in line with official policy and reflected the general mood of militaristic nationalism. In 1942 she travelled to China and Singapore as a member of the "pen squadron," the group of writers recruited by the military authorities to make visits at various warfronts. Because of these activities, she was accused of disloyalty by some members of the Communist Party; she later had further difficulties involving internal disputes and in 1951 was ejected from the Party. These experiences, and the tensions she felt between her commitment to art and to the Communist cause, were to influence her writings in years to come.

During the difficult time prior to the outbreak of World War II, Ineko was increasingly preoccupied with a more personal conflict, namely her identity as a wife and mother and as a writer. This theme is taken up in her novella, *Crimson* (*Kure-*

nai), written in 1936. Heavily autobiographical, the novella analyzes Ineko's own feelings, thoughts and actions during the dark years before the War and chronicles the corrosion of her marriage to Kubokawa. First serialized in *Women's Forum* (*Fujin Kōron*) in 1937, *Crimson* is considered to be one of Ineko's best works. Like Ineko, the protagonist Akiko is a writer who is married to another writer, and the mother of two small children. Akiko's husband complains that the lack of a congenial atmosphere is making him less productive, and Akiko, whose income is an essential part of their household budget, resents the fact that she is made to feel guilty for creating tension instead of harmony. She wonders if she is being punished for being proud of her accomplishments as a writer, and although she experiences great pain and guilt, she also feels entitled to develop her career as a writer.

The central issue of *Crimson* is a question Japanese women writers had never before asked: can the different roles, being a professional woman and a wife and mother, be happily combined? A conflict familiar to us in the post-women's liberation era, it was strikingly new to Ineko's generation. For women like Ineko, whose lovers and husbands were involved in the leftist movement, the gradual realization that the revolutionary theory of sexual equality was largely ignored in practice came with sorrow and a sharp sense of betrayal.

Ineko later wrote another novella, entitled *A Grey Afternoon* (*Haiiro no Gogo*, 1959), in which she again treats the theme of the discord experienced by an intellectual couple; it has a somewhat broader perspective than *Crimson*, involving the interactions of the protagonist's women friends. Ineko's marriage to Kubokawa ended in the spring of 1945.

Ineko's writing was motivated by the urge to reflect on her own life and to discover a new understanding—a mode of writing that has been extremely popular among modern Japanese writers. Ineko's treatment of the mother-child relationship, for example, draws heavily on her own experiences both as a mother and a child. For a poor mother, children are "the light that eases the pain of life," Ineko once wrote, and her own children provided her with a great deal of strength during troubled times. But Ineko's harsh childhood allowed her no illusions about idealized parent-child relationships. In Ineko's fiction, children are given a right to see and judge the adult world according to their own capacities and limitations. Rather than using a child's perspective to give a fresh view of the adult world, as other writers did, Ineko included children in her work because she believed the life and world of a child were equally significant to that of an adult. Though she did not often write exclusively about children, her work shows an understanding of what it is like to be powerless, at the mercy of other people.

The year after World War II ended, Ineko started writing *My Map of Tokyo* (*Watashi no Tōkyō Chizu*). In this impressionistic work reminiscent of wood-cut prints, she recalls her past, tracing the memory of the places she knew as a child and a young woman. The history of both narrator and city come alive in a vivid tableau as the narrator reconfirms the connection between herself and the people around her. The work evokes a sense of nostalgia for what has been lost forever—the narrator's own innocence as well as that of the Japanese people—and an empathy with the nameless individuals who lived, as young Ineko had, in the many corners of Tokyo. Ineko's skills as a writer are at their best as she depicts the ordinary people—workers, housewives, daughters and rootless wanderers—who are trying to live their difficult lives as best as they can.

After completing *My Map of Tokyo*, Ineko continued writing for the next thirty years, producing about eighty books of fiction and essays by 1970. Now in her eighties, she remains active on the Japanese literary scene. A writer whose sympathy for the powerless and the poor helped to give them a voice in literature, Sata Ineko exemplifies the continuing dynamic of art and social commitment.

Y. T.

Crimson

translated by Yukiko Tanaka

The first breath of spring, sweeping across the ground, brought Akiko back to a time long past. The air still cold, a soft breeze touched her cheek invitingly. The buds responded without delay, an accurate gauge of the seasonal change; a sweet scent drifted through the air. All of these signs called forth the memory of an incident that took place in early spring. And this year the arrival of spring once again made her look back with disquieting, bittersweet nostalgia to an event in her life, a life which many changes had made richer.

Her memory was of falling in love with Hirosuke. An experience both painful and exhilarating, because it was the first time she had insisted on her independence—she had joined Hirosuke in his leftist activities. The following year the memory of that spring came to her in the midst of the confusion and excitement of the March Fifteenth Incident. A year later, while on her way to visit the family of a worker victimized in the labor disputes, the memory returned once again. Time passed; Hirosuke fell ill and was temporarily kept from his political work. Sitting by the well, miserable and crying, Akiko had thought, *spring again*, and her heart was filled with sadness.

It was also during springtime that Hirosuke had been arrested. Akiko went to see him at the police station, her newborn daughter on her back. Walking along a street bursting with new greenery, she felt as if her heart were being squeezed. It was a difficult time for her, she had two young children and was involved in revolutionary struggles which were becoming increasingly difficult and dangerous. The recollection of that early spring long ago brought a faint smile to her face, shadowed by her yearnings for Hirosuke, who had been taken away from her and thrown in jail.

Last year, Hirosuke had come back. Akiko had become ill and he was taking care of her. "We've certainly been through a lot together," she had said to him then, a trace of eagerness in her voice.

And this year, spring came around once again. One day Akiko went to see Kishiko, a friend who lived alone in Kami-Ochiai. They took a walk along a dark, quiet street filled with the fragrance of daphne. "There's a very large, sweet-smelling daphne somewhere around here, I remember," Akiko said. "The fragrance is so strong." The two women kept walking, absorbing the pungent sweetness.

"I think it's wrong to think that writers are separated from the masses because of that," Akiko said, returning to their earlier discussion. "In my mind, the writers' position could be explained by making it clear where they stand in their relationships with the masses."

"Hmm . . . I see your point," said Kishiko, nodding slowly a few times.

"However, if you want to write about the masses, you've got to believe that your personal life is directly affecting your work. The work doesn't lie, and so the way we feel about our daily lives is crucial, don't you think so?"

"Hmm . . ." Kishiko nodded again.

"What supports us in times of stagnation like this are our political beliefs. If it weren't for that, there'd be nothing but the routine life of a professional writer for us. But a life like that is quite different from the life of the masses, so how to bridge the gap ought be our major concern, at least in my opinion."

"I think it's important to discuss things like this with other writers. What does Hirosuke say?"

"He's preoccupied with his own studies. He doesn't seem to

be bothered about the kinds of things I've been concerned with lately. For me, everything affects my writing."

"I guess writing fiction is different from writing critical essays. They ought to be the same in the most fundamental sense, though."

"I agree with you there. He and I quarrelled about that once. He wanted to move to Ogikubo, and I said I'd never leave Ōji. The two places are quite different, you know. Hirosuke's reason for moving was so he could be near the Federation Office; he argued that I shouldn't have to be dependent on actual experience for my writing."

"It's a hard time for everybody, no matter what we say. Writers like us are better off than most, though; we can still write or think about writing. The activists must feel that they lost everything when their organizations were disbanded. I guess we're lucky in that sense," Kishiko concluded.

The two women exchanged smiles when they parted, as if to give each other an encouraging pat on the shoulder. Akiko found her husband working in his room upstairs when she returned home.

"Is something wrong?" he asked as he saw her entering the room. "You look troubled."

Akiko realized how completely her talk with Kishiko had affected her mood. "Kishiko and I were discussing some things while we walked." She couldn't snap out of it just like that.

"What things?" Hirosuke asked absently, returning to his work.

"Let me just read this to you," he said, trying to pull her onto his ground. But Akiko was unable to shake her mood. She felt troubled a great deal this spring. She didn't experience the deep emotion which had always stirred her in the past years with the arrival of this season.

- 5 -

At the end of March, Akiko decided to rent a room in a working-class neighborhood east of the River. She found a room in a two-story tenement building, which was actually six houses connected by a single roof and tilted to one side. The building stood on an old factory site adjacent to a marsh. The River, which ran alongside the house, looked black here; purplish-colored oil floated on the surface. Her landlord left early in the morning to work at a dye factory and his wife sewed cotton gloves while she watched her small candy store. An old man who resembled the landlord crouched all day long in a corner of the store.

The town started and ended its days to the sound of sirens. Even late at night the sirens blared, as if they were dogs howling at some disturbance. Akiko felt a peculiar sense of oppression when she heard them. Around noon she would see the young apprentices from nearby factories come out to enjoy the sunshine and chase each other, looking like playful kittens in their round caps and cord pants shining with grease.

Akiko walked along the road by the marsh. The yellowish smoke billowing from the chimneys fell back down upon her, unable to stay in the sky. When the wind blew in, the entire town was assailed by the smog. Nowhere was Akiko able to detect nature's signs telling of the arrival of spring.

Early one morning Akiko went out to the street. Here were the workers, some on bicycles, others pounding along in clogs. And there were others, still in the chophouse, shoveling rice from their bowls into their mouths. The town was busy getting ready for the day's work. Two young women workers, scarves around their faces and wearing slightly soiled aprons, hurried out from the alley. Their feet in their sandals were bare. Though they still covered their heads, they no longer wore socks. Their pale pink feet looked refreshing in the cold air. For Akiko, those bare feet were the first sign of the new season. *Spring is here*, she thought.

Living in this town, Akiko had a chance to think a great deal. In the evenings she walked along the streets, wearing a woolen apron and clogs to do her grocery shopping together with the other residents, who included quite a few Korean women. In her room with the slanted floor and blackened mats she worked and slept alone. But she was not able to write as much or as well as she had hoped. Her mood remained glum.

One evening when it was raining hard, Akiko suddenly felt that she could no longer tolerate living in the rented room. She wrapped herself in a shawl, and after waiting a long time for a taxi, went back to her house in Totsuka. As the taxi approached her destination it seemed to Akiko that the street became brighter, and yet when she arrived at her house she was surprised that it really wasn't that far from the rented room. This set her to thinking about the differences between the two places. She felt that she needed to learn more about the way working-class people lived, but at the same time, she was afraid of losing an appreciation of the life she had cultivated— she was afraid that she could get too accustomed to life in a tenement.

Akiko spent the days of that spring searching her mind, plagued by self-doubt. She was staying at her house, but had decided to find another rented room. On one of these days Kawada Masako, a woman who lived near Kishiko, paid her a visit.

"Kishiko was taken in," she said, clearly upset.

"What? When?" Akiko, who was sitting by the charcoal brazier, stood up.

"This morning."

"I wonder what's happening to her? I hope it's not too bad."

The next morning they came to get Akiko. She was up when they came, so she went upstairs, asking them to wait at the door.

"They've come to take me in," she told Hirosuke, who was still in bed.

"They have?" he said, raising his head right away. He looked serious. Usually he could not wake up that quickly in the morning. "I'm worried. I wonder what it's about"

"I think it's something to do with Kishiko."

"But . . ." he began. They looked at each other silently for a moment, their affection for one another displacing their fear. They heard a voice from downstairs saying that they wanted to inspect the room. Hirosuke got out of his bed.

Akiko got her papers and a hand towel together and left home shortly after that, accompanied by the police. Hirosuke went with them as far as the main street to see her off.

"Where are you going? asked Kōichi, without stopping his play. He was used to being left behind by his mother. His younger sister repeated the question after him.

"Just an errand," said Akiko.

- 6 -

Akiko was detained for forty days and then released. It was already summer, and the colors outside, strong and bright, pierced her eyes. The first thing she wanted to do after her release was to take her children someplace nice. Her sense of relief at getting safely through the interrogation ought to have inspired her to begin some new work, but the only thing she could think about was resting. She couldn't help feeling that the ebb of the leftist movement had affected her own attitude.

At home, Hirosuke seemed to be leading a busy life. When he had been released from prison almost two years ago, he told Akiko that he felt he had lost his place in the home. Now she was feeling the same way. It seemed to her that Hirosuke had taken over the household. She heard his loud voice eagerly talking with his guests; she heard him scolding the maid for neglecting to clean his room; she heard him leaving the house with a visitor. His slender body seemed completely absorbed in work; new books piled up on his desk. He would talk to Akiko about his activities, but she found that she did not enjoying listening to him nor could she give him encouragement.

When Hirosuke had returned from prison and saw how Akiko had fixed up her room, he commented on what a nice room she had made for herself, but he was unable to find a spot in the house where he felt comfortable. Akiko had understood his feelings at the time, and now it was she who suffered from not belonging anywhere. But it was more than that: she felt that the center of gravity in the home had shifted entirely to

Hirosuke. Fear that her daily life—the basis of her writing—
was being eroded became a part of her sense of loss. And she
knew that this was not Hirosuke's will alone—this was a
struggle between a man and a woman to gain power in the
household. Why did she constantly see things in terms of her
sex, she wondered, and felt like crying. She let herself become
more and more withdrawn as the days went on.

Akiko's disposition turned against her husband, changing
from sullen, to harsh, to mean. She used to join him when he
had company, but now she shut herself in her room for reasons unclear except that she didn't want to concern herself
with any of his affairs. She thought about the time when all his
guests—men and women—were her guests, too, and realized
how differently she felt now about so many things. On the
rare occasions when she would join them and make conversation she felt the difference even more keenly than when Hirosuke left without her to go somewhere with his guests. She
wondered why they took for granted that she would stay behind. She began to think there was no other way to establish an
independent life for herself as long as she lived with Hirosuke.

Akiko's emotions, intricately woven out of the threads of
her daily life, began to follow a simple, intense pattern. A
stubborn darkness piled up inside of her. Hirosuke felt it, and
tried to balance her low spirits with the enthusiasm he put into
his own work. He was trying to develop his career by being as
busy as possible. The situation at home didn't seem to bother
him. Once in a while Akiko's ill-tempered response to his
behavior upset him, and he would get angry. She thought that
his anger was justified, and wished that they could be more
harmonious. She felt trapped by the growing conflict inside
herself. In order to let Hirosuke feel free to do whatever he
wanted, she realized that she would have to earn money, not as
a writer, but by doing something else. Hirosuke pursued his
writing single-mindedly and was able to earn only a little
money, forcing Akiko to make up for their shortage of income. She felt frustrated that the money she earned would not
be spent the way she chose, because now it was Hirosuke who
made the decisions. All this was because of his determined

ambition, and although she knew that she also benefited from this, she couldn't help feeling resentful that she hadn't made any plans herself.

"How is your work coming along?" a friend asked.

"Not well at all. I don't really feel like writing lately. I only do it to make ends meet," Akiko answererd despondently.

Hirosuke heard her and couldn't ignore it. He found Akiko's attitude insolent. After all, he was only trying to develop himself in every way possible because he wasn't satisfied with his own work; it seemed to him that she was being self-centered and aggressive. He felt overwhelmed by the stubborn persistence with which Akiko showed her pride. During her absence Hirosuke had realized how dependent he was on her as a close friend, but now he found the pressure of her dark moods unbearable. He wasn't happy at finding himself constantly on guard. They began using words like "losing" and "winning."

What a detestable couple we've become, Akiko thought, and wondered about other wives who viewed the husbands' aspirations as their own. Wives like that did everything possible to promote their husbands' work—encouraged them, tried to inspire them, made them feel good about themselves by feigning helplessness and acting indignant toward others who were critical. That made husbands feel more responsible; they would be strengthened and would drive themselves to work harder.

Hirosuke invited Akiko to go for a walk with him one evening when he came home. It was late, and they passed a noodle cart with a yellow kerosene lamp. They walked along the main street as far as the station and came back. Walking in the cold wind did not bring even a touch of color to Akiko's face which wore a dark, stagnant expression.

"No fun at all to walk with you is it? What's the matter with you, anyway?" Hirosuke said, openly showing his disgust.

"I agree. It's no fun," she snapped. She said it with a coldness that froze any response from Hirosuke. He felt how tightly she had locked herself in. No quarrel developed, and they returned to their separate rooms.

One evening when the moon was full Akiko sat alone by the open window—Hirosuke had gone out somewhere. Although it was already July, the air felt chilly, perhaps because of the pale moonlight. She heard the noises of the children running around downstairs; they were getting ready for bed and the maid was scolding them. She sat as still as a coiled snake, her emotions smoldering; she felt restless, as if something were about to burst inside her. Suddenly, like a person half mad, she stood up and went downstairs.

"Kōichi, come here."

"What is it, Mommy?" Kōichi didn't sound a bit sleepy.

She beckoned him carefully so that Tetsuko wouldn't notice, and her son came out from under the mosquito net in his towel pajamas. He was trying to control himself, but he had a big smile on his face.

"What? What's up?" he asked trying to sound like a grownup.

"Let's go to the River and look at the moon."

"Huum . . . go to see the moon?" he said, and followed his mother out of the house.

The back street, which had only a few street lamps, was filled with the transparent light of the stark blue moon. On the ground the dark shadows of trees were clearly outlined.

"How bright the moon is," Akiko said, holding her son's hand in hers as if she were trying to infuse him with her own feelings.

"Aren't you cold?"

"Cold? No."

They exchanged a few words as they walked side by side, like two adults keeping each other company. Akiko put her arm around her son's shoulders but she didn't look into his face. She was moved by the realization that her son had grown old enough to be company for her, someone who could console her when she was lonely like this at night. That made her wonder if she should pity her son or herself.

Akiko walked quickly, so Kōichi did, too. She started talking like a boy, putting herself on her son's level. Kōichi went on excitedly about the games he played during the day, treating his mother, whose mind was miles away, as an equal. When she realized this, she felt cold-hearted. *I dragged my son out of the house like this, and he, being innocent, is excited. Have I made my children into my possessions?* She shuddered in secret fear.

"Poor kid," she murmured to herself, while responding absent-mindedly to Kōichi. She must not sacrifice her children for the sake of her own needs. Then she asked herself if her life was so empty that she had to rely on her child in order to forget her loneliness. *Shouldn't I thrust myself into a richer life? Isn't that what I really want?* She knew she wanted to live passionately; she wanted to share her life with nameless people.

The moonlight by the River was piercing, and they were able to hear the faint sound of water. They walked along the road where they saw a pile of gravel left on the river bank and a man standing alone on the bridge. The scene seemed to intensify the stillness of the moonlit night.

"Let's sit here for a while," Akiko said, and sat down on the gravel next to Kōichi. She wanted to calm the quivering in her mind.

"The moon is so bright, isn't it, Kōichi?" He lifted his head, and she saw in her son's eyes the reflection of the moon. *Oh, this little boy sitting next to me . . . so small*, she said to herself, filled with love. She picked up a pebble, then held both hands in front of Kōichi, tightly closed.

"Which hand has the pebble?" she asked, shaking her fists.

Surprised at first, but then understanding, Kōichi examined his mother's fists with a serious look on his face. "This one." His finger pressed one of Akiko's closed hands.

"You won, Kōichi. Your turn."

"All right." The child stuck his small fists in front of his mother, trying not to burst out laughing.

"I think it's this one," she said.

"No, you're wrong! It's this one." Kōichi opened the hand which had the pebble. Looking very proud, he lifted his fist to his ear and shook it.

Bathed in the moonlight she felt the chill of the night seep through her cotton kimono and spread through her lower back and around her shoulders. She concentrated on the faint, steady sound of water from the River. The River runs for miles and miles making this sound . . . it curves when it runs into obstacles . . . it winds slowly into Tokyo, flowing through the inner city . . . it runs along dirty back streets behind small houses, sometimes silenced by the noisy streetcars but always reflecting all of the intensity of city life. It finally reaches the Ōkawa, then the ocean. The River keeps flowing . . . it never ends. . . . Occasionally they heard the whistle of the train that runs far north of the River, going beyond Tokyo as far as Kawagoe. . . .

Playing with Kōichi on the gravel, deeply lost in thought, Akiko looked sad. From a distance, under the moon and the arching sky, Kōichi, with his slender nape and rounded back, looked the size of a small monkey.

– 7 –

The summer had promised to be fresh and moist, but now that it had arrived, it had settled in hard. The air was dry; everything on earth seemed to stand perfectly still in an uncanny silence.

Akiko's state of mind was just like this landscape of summer, increasingly desolate and torn apart by the constant friction between her and Hirosuke. They continued to quarrel but afterward she couldn't find any clear-cut reason for their disagreements—they seemed simply triggered by something in the atmosphere. The quarrels would begin over trivial matters, but then, almost always, they would branch out into fundamental issues, and eventually they'd end up criticizing each other's work.

One day Akiko was invited to a round-table discussion of women writers. The topic was what sort of problems a couple might encounter if both were writers and they disagreed in their political views.

"In your case, Mrs. Kakimura, there is always agreement, isn't there?" asked the editor of a literary magazine.

"Well," Akiko started to talk, but she stopped abruptly. The feeling in the room at that moment—the strange silence and cautious glances of the other participants made her feel awkward.

Later she thought that she should simply dismiss this issue from her mind. Still, she couldn't help reflecting over how differently people viewed marital relationships. She remembered the sympathetic looks of the other women writers when she was called upon to respond. She saw that they were reluctant to ask questions of her or make comments, that they tried not to look at her directly. Akiko was annoyed by the pressure of the unspoken idea that remained so deeply embedded in people's minds—even the minds of professional women—the old notion: "the wife follows, the husband leads." It shocked her to realize how simplistic and shallow people were to believe that husband and wife, especially if both were writers, should not disagree on fundamental issues. *My colleagues, my fellow writers, would not, then, understand how I struggle day in and day out in order to live without compromise and deception; they would not understand that Hirosuke and I fight with each other and encourage each other, that we would even attack and refute each other because we are partners.* When her thoughts had reached this point, she couldn't help feeling infuriated.

"When I complete a piece of work and feel totally exhausted," Hirosuke said to Akiko one day when he seemed particularly relaxed and at ease with her, "I think of nothing whatsoever but to sleep. But the fact is," he continued, "there's no such thing as a restful moment in this household, don't you agree? Even though I've finished my work I can't rest, because you're most likely in the middle of your work." He sounded like a spoiled child, and yet she could see how carefully he was trying to not sound selfish.

"You're right about that," Akiko said calmly, but though she agreed, her husband could detect the coldness in her words.

"How are your quarrels with your husband these days?" a

friend asked on another occasion.

"Well, all we do is to acknowledge the reasons for them," Akiko replied derisively. Then, irritated with herself, she added aggressively, under her breath, "That probably means we're making progress, although if that's the case I wonder what the outcome will be."

The friend didn't understand what she'd said, and Akiko caught herself immediately and pretended that she'd made a joke. She shook her head with a sad expression on her smiling face.

"I wonder if you could keep this gentle expression on your face and write at the same time," said Hirosuke one morning when he saw Akiko utterly relaxed. He touched her cheeks and sighed.

"This gentleness is my essence. But in order to keep it, you see, I have to have these other things, too." Akiko looked away, smiling shyly.

Hirosuke gazed at Akiko for a while without saying a word. He seemed to know that if he said something, the gentleness he saw in her face would somehow disappear. At that moment he felt how precious Akiko was to him. *Would I find it so beautiful if this gentleness belonged to someone else, to an ordinary housewife, for example?* he wondered.

Akiko was growing more insistent in her desire to produce better work and was becoming more unsettled. She was increasingly impatient with her lack of ability to transform her passions into actual work. She thought less and less about Hirosuke as time went by. He, too, went through a similar process. Their desire to grow as writers took precedence over their ties to each other.

"I wish I could go abroad. It would be fun to go with Kishiko, and I'd feel safe with her," she said one day, as she stood by the window in her upstairs room, gazing at the glittering sky in the distance. There was yearning in her voice, and a longing to rid her life of pettiness. Hirosuke was there beside her.

"It's not a good idea for two writers to go off together like that. The freshness of your impressions and the originality of your views would inevitably be sacrificed. Without realizing it you'd both restrain yourselves," he said. There was a touch of animosity in his voice.

Akiko was struck by Hirosuke's words, which she felt provided an answer to the doubts she'd been feeling about her relationship to him. Unable to respond right away, she simply nodded, and said to herself: *If that's so, the discord we've been experiencing must be very basic indeed.*

Original title: *Kurenai* (1936).

Uno Chiyo

(1897-   )

BY THE END OF 1922, the year Hirabayashi Taiko and Hayashi Fumiko left their respective native towns to go to Tokyo, Uno Chiyo was already an established writer with two stories published in commercial magazines. Known as a "modern woman" for her colorful relationships with men, her notorious love life both enhanced and hampered her reputation as a writer. However, her spectacular financial success in publishing certainly contributed to a more positive image of women writers in pre-war Japan. Though not a prolific writer, Chiyo produced several excellent works of fiction.

A hard-working and ambitious student, Chiyo was at the top of her class in her all-girls high school. Her teachers, like those in many other girls' schools of that time, were small-minded conservatives who prohibited the students from reading anything other than textbooks. She was fond of reading and writing and, in spite of strong discouragement both at school and at home, maintained an interest in literature. Chiyo aspired to become a high school teacher and studied diligently for her qualifying examination—she is said to have copied nearly one hundred textbooks in a month to prepare herself. But for whatever reasons, she never took the exam, becoming instead a substitute teacher in a village primary school. This was a pattern that was to repeat itself again and again in Chiyo's life: a project or goal she had pursued single-mindedly would suddenly be abandoned in favor of a new interest.

Chiyo quickly earned the disapproval of the primary school principal by her own unconventional appearance—her heavily made-up face, her brightly colored kimonos. Totally unconcerned with what people might think of her, she fell in love with a young fellow teacher, despite the unwritten rule against

such liaisons. Caring neither about the rules nor her reputation, Chiyo openly sent a student to her lover's room to deliver love letters she had written during class.

   The threat of being fired over such incidents didn't deter
Chiyo, but when she realized that her lover was more concerned with these social conventions than he was with her, she
decided to go to Tokyo to seek her fortune. For ambitious girls
like Chiyo, Tokyo symbolized a chance to succeed, to put
one's aspirations into action. Chiyo did not shirk hard work or
find it debilitating and she had a number of different jobs. Her
bohemian life did not last long, however, because soon she fell
in love with and was married to her cousin, a man totally
reliable and financially secure. The couple moved to the city of
Sapporo, where he worked in an insurance company. It was
during a long, severe winter in Sapporo that Chiyo began
thinking of writing for publication. Her only previous writing
experience had been during her high school days when she had
joined a local group producing a small mimeographed literary
journal.

   Chiyo's decision to write was probably less an urge for creative expression than it was a desire to make some extra income. She had already been working as a seamstress, saving
the money and investing it in a boarding house, which she was
running very efficiently. She enjoyed being a middle-class
housewife and a hard-working business woman, and one day
it occurred to her that she could increase her income by writing stories at night, while she waited for her husband's late
return. Writing fiction was therefore another of Chiyo's many
impulses and she pursued it with characteristic determination.

   Chiyo's first story, which she wrote without much preparation and with no guidance, was sent to a national paper and
received the first prize in a competition. She entered another
competition right away and was successful again. Greatly encouraged, she wrote a much longer piece and sent it to *Chūō
Kōron* (*Central Forum*), the most reputable general magazine
that also published fiction. Her first story had been about a
prostitute; this one, "To Open a Grave" (*Haka o Abaku*), was a
protest against the establishment. Based on her experience of

teaching in the village school, the story exposed the hypocrisy and small-mindedness of educators. Chiyo must have had great expectations for this novella, because after she had not heard from *Central Forum* for six months, she decided to make the several-hundred-mile trip to Tokyo to find out about it. It was the spring of 1922; Chiyo was twenty-five years old. She never returned to Sapporo where her husband awaited her.

To Chiyo's surprise, "To Open a Grave" had already gone to press for the May issue of *Central Forum*, and, to her even greater surprise, she was paid nearly four hundred yen. With this money she visited her stepmother, taking many gifts, and then decided to settle in Tokyo for a period to write and make more money. The following year she wrote another story, a number of essays for commercial journals, and published her first book. Chiyo's unusually fortunate start, without a single instance of discouragement, not even a beginner's period of trial and error, caused jealous suspicions among some writers. There were even rumors that Chiyo had had sexual relations with Takita Choun, the editor of *Central Forum*. Chiyo herself felt that Takita, who had known her when she was working at a restaurant near his office, was impressed by her story precisely because it was the work of a waitress. She also knew that the demand for her writing was great because of the scarcity of work by women writers, and she soon found out that she was able to publish light stories and essays whenever she needed money. Years later, Chiyo wrote an autobiographical essay, "A Genius of Imitation" (*Mohō no Tensai*), about her youth and these early days of her writing career.

Although Chiyo produced quite a few short stories and essays in the first ten years of her career, it was not until 1933 that she published her first significant work, a novel entitled *Confession of Love* (*Iro Zange*). Chiyo had in the meantime dissolved her five-year marriage with Ozaki Shirō, her second husband, and started quite a different life with Tōgō Seiji, a well-known painter who had lived in France for many years and who had once been involved in a sensational double suicide attempt. The couple met when Chiyo visited Tōgō to interview him about the suicide attempt—she was writing a novel with a double suicide scene and needed information. The next day, they decided to live together. The novel *Confession of Love*, which established Chiyo as a serious writer, is largely based on the suicide story Tōgō told Chiyo. Although Chiyo characteristically made a self-effacing statement that if the work was any good it was because of Seiji's skillful narration, it stands out as one of the finest novels treating the theme of love written in the pre-World War II period.

The novel's story is told by a weak-willed, apathetic artist who is unwillingly involved with two women: a capricious and willful daughter of an upper-class family, who has taken a fancy to him and then suddenly changes her mind, and a pretty but spoiled girl who elopes with her former boyfriend after she has married the narrator. He then becomes involved with a third woman, Tsuyako, an innocent but impassioned young woman who attempts suicide both out of despair and in protest against her parents, who object to her relationship with the artist. The novel, at once lyrical and intellectual, is significant for its accurate portrayal of Japanese society during the late 1920s—a time of instability and confusion—as well as for its female protagonists who insist on choosing their own futures yet still lack the means to financial independence.

Life with Seiji lasted nearly five years. Chiyo soon found herself spending most of her time and energy selling Seiji's paintings rather than working on her writing. She began to feel a strong need to have her own place where she could live and write on her own—the same urge she had felt before leaving her husband, Ozaki Shirō. These experiences of separation provided material and momentum for her fiction and followed a pattern which Chiyo would repeat a third time in 1964, when she was sixty-seven years old and dissolving her fourth marriage. This break-up produced *To Sting* (*Sasu*), a novel very different from *Confession of Love* in style and theme.

In the summer of 1939, when the country was escalating its war effort to exploit China, Chiyo ventured into the publication of a fashion magazine for young women, *Style* (*Sutairu*)—the first fashion magazine in Japan. With the help of a young journalist and aspiring novelist named Kitahara Takeo, the magazine became successful, and Chiyo was married to Kitahara the same year. After a few years of forced closure because of the paper shortage during World War II, Chiyo and Kitahara started publishing *Style* again in 1946, this time with even greater success. The magazine, with its colorful pictures of young women on the cover, was enthusiastically received by Japanese readers, who had been getting along with little entertainment of any kind during the war years. Chiyo then put her energy into designing kimonos and established a design institute in 1949. She made a great deal of money through these successful business ventures and for some time enjoyed building fabulous houses and traveling to Europe. All was lost, however, with the bankruptcy of her magazine's publishing house in 1959. Several similar magazines had started by then, making the competition stiff. Having devoted most of her time to designing kimonos, Chiyo wrote little during this period except for short essays on clothes and food and an occasional travel account.

Despite the financial setbacks and preoccupation with her business, Chiyo did not give up her creative endeavors. She started a literary magazine with Kitahara a few years after starting *Style*, which she called *The Literary Style (Buntai)*. For this magazine she wrote her most accomplished work, a novella entitled *Ohan* (tr. 1961), which took her ten years to complete. The novella is narrated by a man caught between two types of passion, one represented by his wife, Ohan, a passive woman who, though forced to leave her husband, will not easily give him up, and Okayo, the proprietor of a restaurant and an ex-geisha, who wants to dominate him. The novella is based on the story told to her by the owner of a small antique shop in a remote town in Shikoku, where Chiyo frequently went during the war to collect stories from a famous Bunraku doll maker. Once again Chiyo used actual incidents as the basis of her fiction and shaped it into a near-perfect art form. She received the 1958 Women's Literary Award for this work.

Chiyo has written repeatedly about herself, hinting at se-

crets of her long, successful life and career. In a short but revealing story called "Happiness" (*Kōfuku*, 1971; tr. 1982), the
narrator, a thinly disguised Chiyo, says that she can find pleasure in things that might appear odd to other people; standing
in front of the mirror, naked after her bath, she sees, with the
help of her failing eyes, a body resembling Botticelli's Venus.
In such a way she collects "fragments of happiness one after
another." Like this narrator, Chiyo knows that satisfaction
comes from pursuing the objects of her affection; she feels she
has achieved independence from the world of disquieting affairs.

Uno Chiyo's inner strength and integration of life and art
sustained her over many decades of writing. The painstaking
care with which she approached her craft distinguished her
from other writers—though she modestly shrugged off such
recognition. In 1977, when Chiyo turned eighty, the first of
the twelve-volume collection of her works was published. She
stated on this occasion that after nearly four decades, she still
looked forward to more years of writing. She did indeed publish two more books in 1984, a testimony to her enduring
dedication as an artist.

Y. T.

A Genius of Imitation

translated by Yukiko Tanaka

I was born in Iwakuni in Yamaguchi Prefecture on November 28, 1897; I am now thirty-eight years old. Influenced by the spirit of the times and my surroundings, I grew up a child who wanted to go to the battlefields despite my sex: I aspired to be a kind, gentle nurse like Florence Nightingale or an officer as brave as Jean of Arc. All the songs we learned at school were about war. I still remember "Six Hundred Miles from Nagato Bay," and "Marching through the Snow; Treading on the Ice," and can sing them even now. Miniature books of war songs, filled with tiny print, sold for five sen. Later, slender song books of a slightly larger format were published one after another. Singing the lines of the songs, particularly those written in vernacular language, like "In the Burning Sunset," or "Only the Clock's Ticking Away," I was touched; I could imagine the gusty wind blowing over the battlefields many miles away. It was these war songs, now that I think about it, that introduced me to literature.

Magazines and newspapers were forbidden me by my father, who was very strict. I read them secretly in the outhouse anyway, not minding when my bottom was chilled by the cold air creeping up from underneath the toilet. The newspapers in those days serialized modern stories such as "One's Own Sin" or "A Bride's Abyss." I didn't quite understand what these stories were about, but the mystery of the adult world swelled in my imagination like a dangerous boil. I don't remember how many times I was spanked after being caught by my father when he came to use the outhouse. I thought the world of fiction was endlessly fascinating, and the stricter my father was, the sneakier I became. I looked for all kinds of ways to read stories. Once, I discovered piles of very old newspapers and some magazines called *A Flower of the Capitol* in the corner of the storehouse; I read them by the dim light from the window until it was dark. There were also some old letters addressed to my father. He was a man who had a reputation as a ladies man in his younger days, and I imagined that these letter were from women. They were rolled up, with red borders at the top and the bottom of the paper, like the letters Okaru wrote in *The Legend of Chūshingura*. My father must have thought that caution was necessary lest his daughter follow in his footsteps. If so, he was wrong in his disciplinary approach because I grew up wanting to do whatever he had forbidden.

My father died when I was sixteen. After offering their condolences, the neighbors said to my mother and me, "But I'm sure your life will be a lot easier now," and they even congratulated themselves on his death. My father was not, in retrospect, like a character one would expect to find in Japanese fiction, but more like someone out of the novels of Balzac or Dostoevsky. I cried bitterly, but somehow I was happy at the same time, thinking that I could now do whatever I wanted.

At the all-girls high school I attended, we also were forbidden to read newspapers and magazines, but there it was easy to get around the rules. I read quite a few magazines—*The Third Empire, Bluestocking*. Deeply stimulated by a then fashionable motto, "In antiquity, woman was the sun," my friends at the school and I thought that we might really be the sun. We published a small magazine, as many literary-minded young people did in those days, featuring poems and essays of an abstract nature. This magazine was soon discovered by the teacher, and one afternoon we were summoned by the principal. "I trust this writing doesn't reflect what you girls really believe," the principal scolded us gravely in the cold room. The magazine on his desk looked pathetic, its pages flapping in the wind from the window. Someone started sobbing, and then all of us joined her. We didn't know why we were sad but the sadness seemed to belong to a sphere beyond our ordinary world; we liked words such as "exalted" and "noble." The principal's ideas about discipline proved to be no more effective than my father's; soon after this dressing-down we joined another literary group, outside the school, that published a typeset magazine. I also met people who wrote novels in which lovers talked like city people. Aspiring writers in this group got together and went to the town photographer to have their picture taken: young men in straw hats or holding walking sticks; women clasping artificial chrysanthemums or a parasol.

I finished high school and immediately started teaching at an elementary school in a village four miles from town. The salary was eight yen a month with an end-of-the-year bonus of fifty sen. So I became a teacher. I went to the school wearing white powder on my face and a long, blue *hakama* skirt over my tight-sleeved kimono that was adorned with a wide, decorative cord at the wrists, an outfit remniscent of the one worn by the ancient hero, Prince Yamato Takeru. I rented a room in a farm house by the river, not far from school. There I began my independent life.

I bought rice and soap with the money I earned, and kept a ledger. My total expenses for the month came to about three-and-a-half yen, so at the end of every month I had more than four yen left. A life that cost three-and-a-half yen. . . . Each day I got up early in the morning and prepared black beans for the breakfast meal. I roasted them in an earthenware pan and poured soy sauce over them right away. I ate these beans with rice for lunch and for dinner as well. I was a very strict teacher. On the wide, open playground I led the children's gymnastic exercises with lively commands; the wind from the sea would blow through the top branches of poplar trees and flutter the soiled aprons of the children and the hem of my skirt. An old man used to lean against the fence, watching us while he waited for his grandchild to finish school.

After school I would play the organ for a while and sing

songs in a low, expressive voice. Yes, I was in love. It was joyful to be young, to be alive. Instead of thinking I might be the sun, I now felt I was a butterfly. I stopped writing verses and essays. I had no time to spare. Instead of writing about my emotions, I acted upon them. I was in love just like the characters in the stories in the typeset magazine we had published. I thought I had no need to write any more.

That was when I was eighteen, and between then and the year I turned twenty-six, I didn't write a single line. I worked every day; I was in love. Days came and went. My life and my love, which was so joyous in the beginning, gradually became distressing. One day I packed and left my home town on a ferry boat. When the boat pulled away and the whistle sounded, I saw in the distance the railroad tracks, the pine trees on the faraway hills and my mother standing by the shore in the morning mist.

I arrived in Tokyo with a small bundle of belongings and an umbrella. What was I to do? First I had to find a job. I was young and had plenty of time later to do what I really wanted, I told myself. Every day I went out and looked around. There were all kinds of jobs, but I had to feed myself and needed to earn money right away. Hotels and restaurants, both Japanese and Western-style, were the main places where women who had nothing but their able bodies could work. I became a waitress at a hotel restaurant, and later at another restaurant; I also worked as a clerk at a publishing house, as a tutor, as an assistant to the editor of a textbook on flower arrangement. If it had been a Hollywood movie, I would have met a rich, good-looking man who would have taken me to a nice seaside or mountain resort. But the only men who appeared in my life were poor, uninteresting, and short. So I had to continue working till one of my lovers, who managed to graduate from the university and get a position in Sapporo, sent for me. I quit my job and got on the train.

It snowed a lot in Sapporo. In the room with the curtains drawn and coals burning in the stove, I knit socks for my

husband. I became a good housewife. My husband, a cashier
for an insurance company, played pool after work. Listening
to the sleigh bells, I thought it was simply wonderful to be a
housewife, that I had nothing to worry about. Now, I told
myself, I could start my studies so that I could become a "significant" woman. I got out pen and paper. From my husband's bookshelves I chose a collection of essays on women by
Babel and began translating it. I might become a writer like
Hiratsuka Raichō or Yamakawa Kikue. . . . My husband returned home late one night and looked at my work. "What's a
'Sukopenhuauer'?" he asked. I told him it was the name of a
person, Schopenhauer, and he laughed, loudly, for a long
time. I put my pen down and sighed. What a long winter. . . . I
drew all the curtains and knitted socks again.

   One day I thought about a customer who used to eat at the
restaurant where I worked in Tokyo. All the waitresses called
him "Kintarō." This "Kintarō," whose real name was Takita
Cyogyū, came to the restaurant every day at noon, crossing
the street from the bank building where, on the third floor, the
Chūō Kōron publishing house was located. He would eat a
five-course lunch in fifteen minutes, gulp a beer, throw a fifty-
sen coin tip onto the silver-plated serving tray, and hurry out
of the restaurant. I bought many things with those fifty-sen
coins back in those days. That's it, I said to myself; I should try
to see if Kintarō would give me fifty sen again. And I started
writing. I wrote everyday. I wasn't sure if my work could be
called a novel; I just wrote, skipping the parts I didn't know
how to handle. The writing came easily, and when I had finished about one hundred pages I gave it a serious title: "To
Open a Grave." It was a story with a clear theme and had a
young idealistic teacher, clearly resembling the author, as the
heroine; it depicted the heroine's struggles against the public
education system, which did not treat the handicapped children with due consideration. Even after I had sent the manuscript off, I couldn't calm myself. I might be able to become
like Cyūjyō Yuriko, I thought. "Like" was my mode of thinking: I first sought a model, and then tried to become "like" that
person. I was like a girl who covets a pretty ball belonging to

another girl. I waited a long time for a reply. Violets bloomed
on the ground that had been covered by snow during the long
winter.

I'll go to Tokyo and check it out myself, I decided one day.
Kintarō might have misplaced my precious manuscript somewhere on a shelf. I got on the train. The whistle sounded as the
train left the platform, where my husband stood seeing me off.
It was hard to leave my gentle husband behind, but I felt I had
to go. I cried when I no longer was able to see him through the
heavy smoke.

I went straight to the Chūō Kōron publishing house from
the station. When Mr. Takita saw me he tossed a newly printed magazine onto the desk. "Here it is," he said. It took some
time for me to understand what he meant. My story had been
published in the May issue of the magazine. It would be in the
bookstores in a few days. As I thought about this, my heart
started pounding and a strange feeling of apprehension filled
my abdomen. My story is published, I said to myself, and left
the room without even thanking Mr. Takita. I ran down the
stairs. Whom should I tell first? Outside on the street I glanced
at the restaurant where I used to work, and then started running. I now had three hundred and some yen in my pocket,
money I had earned from the first story I ever submitted. And
yet no one knew about me; Tokyo was a big city. How marvelous life was. In my imagination I saw the entire manuscript
as if it were written on a block of wood. I'd finally become a
significant woman. Kintarō had given me money again, only
this time an enormous sum. Mr. Takita had probably read my
manuscript out of curiosity . . . a waitress he used to know had
written a story. A waitress who writes a story, I thought, had a
definite advantage over, say, a young woman from a good,
middle-class family. In the same sense, I now feel lucky, being
born a woman.

This feeling of being lucky, however, had nothing to do
with genuine good fortune. Although I had become a writer
overnight, I didn't know what to write next. I had yet to find
my model. I managed to recall works by Takayama Cyogyū
and *Nature and Life*, which I had read some eight years before.

Should I write like that? No matter what I was going to write, I had first to decide: to write "like" whom? So this poor writer began reading. I read whatever caught my eye, one book after another, works of both Japanese and foreign authors. Like a housewife who became suddenly rich, I had to learn to put a costume on properly, in a hurry, without anyone knowing about it. And after a while I was able to produce a few pieces, one of which resembled Strindberg; another, Satomi Ton. I also wrote a Chekhovian story. My talent seemed colorfully varied, like a rainbow, and it appeared I was a born writer. Women are forever concerned with what to wear, and so, pre-occupied with what I should put myself into, I came to believe that those borrowed outfits were my own, that I could change from one to the other depending on my mood. I became better known, and I aspired to be like Tamura Toshiko, like George Sand. I was so absorbed in myself that I forgot about returning to my home in Hokkaidō where violets were blooming—in fact I didn't even realize that I'd forgotten. It was hard to believe that the woman who had cried in the Tokyo-bound train and I were the same person. A woman's memory is conveniently flexible.

Soon I had a house built in a suburb of Ōmori, and I lived there with my new husband, a writer named Ozaki Shirō. I was happy, and I wrote all day long. My daily life was so calm and quiet that I could hear the breeze outside my window. I meticulously described every detail of my life. My dog got sick and I wrote about it in a story; a new neighbor moved in next door and I wrote about *that*. When I wrote a line, I'd turn to my new husband and ask how he would have written it, for I had now decided that he—and only he—was my teacher. I saw life through the glasses of this teacher; I thought his glasses were marvelous. When the result seemed to fit his taste more than mine, I felt relieved. I read the books my husband read and used his pen to write my stories. My life became indistinguishable from my work, and I became a mere wife in fact and fiction. The pieces I wrote sat still, hunching their shoulders and contemplating me like a demon in the darkness.

How ludicrous it is that I act like a wife in my career as a

writer. I should, at least, have borrowed a telescope from my
husband once in a while instead of always using his eyeglasses.
I feel helpless even now, wondering how much longer I'll
continue this imitating. When I think about it, I get terribly
discouraged, even in my proudest moments. My Mr. Strindberg, my Mr. Chekhov, and my Mr. Schnitzler. . . . I am thirty-eight years old, I've been writing for twelve years, and I
don't know who I really am. Now I am the wife of a painter,
Tōgō Seiji. These days I wear French-inspired, light-colored
clothes instead of those somber Scandinavian outfits I wore a
few years back. I don't remember when I made the switch, and
when I spread my old clothes out to air, I can't help being
amazed that I did, in fact, wear them once. Now I'm trying to
become like Madame Nowaie, and so glamorous hotels and
parties, horseracing, fickle wives and good-looking gentlemen abound in my stories. "What car should this woman be
driven in?" I ask my husband. My stories smell of perfume
worn by fancily dressed young women.

Someday, when I am older, will I be able to get rid of this
impulse, this wanting to be "a good wife," without feeling
lost? Would I then be able to write my own story? I don't wish
not to be a woman, but I'd certainly like to be a woman whose
sense of purpose comes from within.

Original title: *Mohō no Tensai* (1936).

Okamoto Kanoko

(1889–1939)

OKAMOTO KANOKO WAS A SINGULAR WOMAN; both her personality and her fiction, which she started writing at age forty-seven, defy comparison. There is an aura of mystery over her turbulent life and sudden death as there is in her written works. Kanoko's art is essentially Romantic; her fiction contains passages of unparalleled beauty and an underlying sense of awe. Her vibrant personality, her belief in the strength of the female psyche and the life-giving properties of a woman's passion are clearly represented in her poetry and prose.

Kanoko began writing *waka*, traditional Japanese poetry, when she was in her teens; her first collection was published when she was twenty-three. The eldest daughter of an old and wealthy family from a city near Tokyo, Kanoko was named after an ancestor who had restored the family from the verge of financial destruction. She was treated with a sense of reverence and admiration by her parents and other members of the household. A sickly child, she was reared by a nurse who looked upon her as a princess of the feudal time; she was pampered but also tutored strictly in all areas of accomplishment necessary for a young woman of an upper-class family, such as *waka*, Japanese and Chinese literary classics, calligraphy, music and dance. Kanoko's father, not especially talented in any field, was a man of considerable moral integrity; and her mother, kind and well-educated, recognized her daughter's exceptional qualities. Her older brother, who also worshiped her, introduced Kanoko to the pleasures and satisfaction of writing. Historically, women in Kanoko's family had been deeply revered, and this perhaps explains the special care she received as a child. The narcissistic tendencies evident in Kanoko's work can be traced back to her exceptional childhood and the adoration she came to expect.

While in her twenties, Kanoko dedicated herself to the study of Buddhism, an interest she pursued for more than a decade. She became well known as a scholar of an esoteric school of Buddhism, lecturing extensively and even publishing a few books on the subject. According to her own statements, she approached Buddhism in the search for a release from her failing marriage, and in the hope of finding the will to start a new life.

When she first turned to Buddhism, she had been married for six years and had borne three children, two of whom had died within their first year. She had also suffered from a severe neurosis that hospitalized her for several months. Her husband, Ippei, was a poor art student when she married him. It was a great strain on young Kanoko, the overprotected daughter of a well-to-do family, to manage the household on next to nothing and to get along with her husband's family. Matters did not improve when Ippei began earning money, for he started drinking and spending his time in the local redlight district. This was a bitter pill for Kanoko to swallow, since Ippei had been the most ardent of suitors; only after a persistent courtship had he managed to persuade Kanoko and her mother—who feared an ordinary marriage would make her sensitive and high-strung daughter unhappy—that he would be a worthy husband.

The strains in the marriage reached a crisis when Ippei deserted the family. Kanoko, totally incapable of taking care of such everyday matters as securing food, was left utterly helpless. It is said that she and her small son sometimes went hungry for days at a time. Her father was at that time in serious financial trouble and her mother and older brother were no longer living. It didn't occur to Kanoko to tell anyone directly about her predicament; the closest she came was through the *waka* poems she was writing for the women's journal *Bluestocking* (*Seitō*). Fortunately Ippei abandoned his reckless ways and returned to his family. He had become a rather successful political cartoonist and felt that he could further restore his self-confidence by helping Kanoko's own career along.

Kanoko herself eventually developed a number of love affairs, which continued off and on throughout her life and bore a certain relationship to her creative activity. Kanoko fell in love easily, particularly with young, good-looking men, and as it happened, the Okamoto household was often extended to include young, single men. For example, when Kanoko and Ippei left for an extended trip to Europe with their son at the end of 1929, two young men accompanied them: one a surgeon whom Kanoko had met and fallen in love with at the time of an operation, the other a university student entrusted with the Okamoto's finances. When she fell in love, Kanoko usually made no attempt to express her passion to the other person but instead secretly suffered until her emotions became overwhelming. The thrill, the pain, and the inner turmoil, all of which she seemed to savor, were a part of her artistic inspiration.

Kanoko's interest in fiction writing and her resolve to learn its art paralleled her dedication to the study of Buddhism. Although she had been writing *waka*, she felt constricted by the brevity of its thirty-one syllables and decided that fiction could more adequately express the complexity of her soul. She spent ten diligent years studying the art of fiction, which included the extended trip to Europe (with stays in Paris, London and Berlin) that was undertaken for her education as well as for her son Taro, an aspiring painter.

Kanoko's first published story, "The Crane was Frail" (*Tsuru wa Yamiki*), is based on her encounters with Akutagawa Ryūnosuke, a writer who killed himself over his irreconcilable conflict between his life and art. It wasn't widely hailed but did receive excellent reviews in *Literary World* (*Bungakkai*), a journal published by the young writers who started the literary trend of Neo-Sensualism. Her second work, entitled "Mother's Love" (*Boshi Jojō*, 1937; tr. 1982), established Kanoko as a fiction writer. It was published in 1937, twenty years after she had begun publishing *waka* poems, essays and articles on Buddhism. An autobiographical story, "Mother's Love" describes Kanoko's inner world during the dark days when Ippei deserted her, her love for Taro, and her involvement in a love

affair. Written in an often lavish style, it conveys a strange
mixture of melancholy, desolation and emotional turmoil. In
the same year Kanoko published "The Story of an Old Geisha" (*Rōgi Shō*, tr. 1985), one of her finest stories. The narrative revolves around an accomplished, middle-aged geisha
who indulges in supporting a young man in her home. The
man, who dreams of becoming an inventor, begins to feel his
energy being drained and tries to escape from her. Each time
he threatens to run away, the geisha feels renewed vitality.
Two other stories Kanoko wrote about the same time, "A
Floral Pageant" (*Hana wa Tsuyoshi*) and "Goldfish in Turbulence" (*Kingyo Kakuran*), treat the same theme—a woman's
inner strength and vigor overpowers a man, who withers and
dies. Keiko, the heroine of "A Floral Pageant," seems to sap
the final strength from her dying lover, which feeds her creative powers. In "Goldfish in Turbulence" this theme is further
developed: the heroine, Masako, is a young, exceptionally
pretty girl embodying ideal beauty; her lover, Fukuichi, is
slowly overwhelmed by his obsession to create a new breed of
goldfish that can match Masako's celestial beauty.

The images of women in Kanoko's fiction are always very
powerful. Her female characters are strong and vital, beautiful
and passionate, and they very often overpower the men who
are drawn to them. Kanoko was often compared with the male
writer Tanizaki Junichiro because of her aestheticism, particularly her elevation of physical beauty to the metaphysical level.
The beauty Kanoko worshipped, however, was not abstract
but concrete and earthly. Unlike Tanizaki's female protagonists, who were often the reflection of the author's obsessive
adoration, Kanoko's central characters were women conscious of their strength; they are heroines in a true sense.

An intensely private person, Kanoko remained a puzzle to
her contemporaries. Her public image was that of both a complex artist and an immature, elusive narcissist. Ippei helped to
reinforce the mysterious image of Kanoko by defining her as
his Beatrice. He believed that Kanoko embodied creative inspiration and eternal youth and did everything he could do to
assist her writing—for instance, by creating a certain mood in

her room where she wrote. There were critics and writers who saw intelligence and depth in Kanoko's fiction with its rich imagery, but others found it merely self-indulgent. The acceptance of Kanoko's work was partly hampered by her mysterious and misunderstood persona, a good example of the phenomenon, unfortunately not rare, in which the facts of a writer's personal life become the overriding interest.

Kanoko died suddenly at age fifty, only two years after her first work of fiction was published. A large number of manuscripts, including several novels, were discovered after her death; many were published posthumously in 1939 and 1940. In some of these works she developed the idea that the essential nature of women was symbolized by water, equating virginity with a spring of pure water in the depth of a mountain; after passing through the middle stage of a full-flowing river, the water merged with the eternal sea. This concept of the female sex as a life-giving, ever-flowing force was the most positive view of female sexuality taken by any Japanese woman of Kanoko's generation. As in the majority of her writing, the centrality of women's sexuality and the strength of the female psyche create Kanoko's thematic underpinnings. Kanoko's voice, distinctively female yet completely unique, remains one of the most significant in Japanese literature of the twentieth century.

Y. T.

A Floral Pageant

translated by Hiroko Morita Malatesta

The water in the large aquarium was clouded with algae, looking heavy as lead. A pair of calico goldfish stopped their graceful swim and sank quietly to the bottom, sensitive to the heaviness of the atmosphere. Together they looked out, as if in
formation, their tails hidden in the dark green swirl of water.
A ceramic zebra with amber eyes stood next to the tank, pressing its nose against the dewy glass. A potted plum sat on the lid
of the tank, scattering delicate pink petals. The powerful sta-
mens stood out from the branches like pins on a cushion.

Mionoya Keiko watched the pair of goldfish in the tank,
marveling at how quickly they reacted to any change in the
weather. She was the leader of a modern movement in the art
of flower arrangement, giving lessons to wives and daughters
of well-to-do families. Having finished with her pupils for the
day, she gathered the flowers and branches left over from the
day's session and made an arrangement in a bamboo vase for
herself. She regarded her work for a while, and then, noticing
the changing weather outside her window, turned to gaze at
how it affected her goldfish.

The sky turned dark and ominous. As it began to rain, a
sudden flash of lightning illuminated the sunken charcoal
hearth.

"Goldfish, zebra, flowers, lightning—a scene to delight the
senses of a symbolist poet." Keiko spoke half to herself and

half to her niece Senko, who had just entered the room. She thought for a moment that when she herself left France, there were still those survivors of the *fin de siècle* who kept composing lines in this vein.

Senko poured water into the bamboo vase that contained Keiko's unfinished work.

"Today is the thirtieth, tomorrow is the last day of the month," Senko said. "Perhaps you should bring some money to Mr. Kobuse tonight."

Kobuse was a distant relative of Keiko's, a painter who at one time had studied oil painting with her under the same teacher. His works did not sell and his health was failing, so Keiko had provided for him for years.

Keiko took the kerchief off the lap of her kimono, gathering the remnants of her arrangement. Senko's constant concern for the sickly Kobuse touched Keiko. She wondered if Senko was secretly in love with him. Keiko then loosened her kimono a bit at the throat, twisted her full waist and relaxed her *obi* a little with her right thumb. The stiff silk of the *obi* squeaked.

"My, that was uncomfortable. Sometimes it's hard to behave myself in front of the students. Won't you bring in some green tea, Senko?"

A loud clap of thunder rumbled through the room, which was done in the style of a tea cottage. The echo then grew distant. Keiko had some tea and sweets with Senko, who was an apprentice as well as her niece. Keiko then scooped up envelopes from a lacquer stand inlaid with gold and wrapped them in her kerchief. The bundle contained all her students' payments for the month.

"Well, I think I'll go see my young man now," Keiko teased, to see how Senko would react. Senko looked around the room, frowning.

"Don't ever say such a thing, even in fun. What if someone heard you?" Keiko could detect nothing more in Senko's tone than a genuine concern for her aunt and teacher.

"It's only very natural, you see," said Keiko a bit sadly, "for a single woman to joke like that."

Keiko's sadness, however, melted away in the soft spring

rain that fell on her umbrella as she walked out the front door.
Fearful of gossip, Senko had tried to dissuade her from visiting
Kobuse during the day. But stretching her tall, statuesque
body, Keiko looked back at Senko and said:

"It's best to meet the rumors head on by marching out in
broad daylight."

With trusting eyes Senko watched her aunt's figure recede.
She felt that beneath the gentle and youthful exterior her aunt
possessed a strength sufficient to overcome any difficulties.
Imagining herself imbued with the same strength, she called
out to the kitchen cheerfully: "Look at all those green berries
out front! They are so easy to miss on the bush."

Even before the old housekeeper had a chance, Kuwako,
another apprentice, and a houseboy came running out to the
front yard.

Keiko was walking down a hilly street in an uptown section
of Tokyo where shops and well-to-do homes seemed to fight
for space. Lined with old cherry trees, the street led to a hollow. Patches of snake's beard with lily-like flowers grew along
the path, and above them rose a number of stately garden trees
covered with vines and creepers. It appeared that there was
once an entrance to a large, mangificent garden in this area,
which had since been divided into lots, and now only this road
remained. The tight combination of old, gnarled trunks and
thin, muscular branches suggested to Keiko garden gates
made of steel and wrought iron.

The wiry branches of the steely old trunks were covered
with pale yellow-green of new leaves. Coming down into the
hollow, Keiko suddenly thought of Gorgonzola cheese. The
blue-green mold that bloomed in the cracks of decaying fat in
the cheese seemed to her so fresh and sensuous. The world
contained things, thought Keiko, that were so inexplicably
beautiful that they scarcely seemed real.

Walking by herself in lonely places, she sometimes had a
sudden craving for rich, strong things like cheese. Since going
abroad her palate had been changed by Western food; she felt
amazed that she could still enjoy green tea and simple sweets

with Senko at her studio.

The rain had stopped and the sun poured down rays of yellow roses in funnel shapes. What remained of a thorny hedge gave off a strong, greenish odor. Keiko looked down fondly at the young, red thorns, sharp as a needle, yet somehow like a baby in their color and shape.

"Prick me if you dare."

She pushed the tip of one thorn with her forefinger; resisting slightly, it bent down. As she pushed harder, the outer skin stretched as if to burst, and the inside wrinkled. Suddenly, Keiko thought she heard the cry of a baby, as if the thorn were crying out in pain. She withdrew her hand.

Thirty-eight years old, Keiko was in her prime; she felt guilty that she had not yet borne any children. At times she heard the cries of those formless children she had chosen not to bear. Hallucinations of this nature were not uncommon; she felt persecuted, that she had suffered innumerable hurts and wrongs in her life. A sudden, overwhelming unhappiness swept over Keiko. She wanted to run to Kobuse's house like a small girl, wanted the younger man to console her and offer her something delicious. She swallowed hard, and tears ran down her face.

Her umbrella closed, Keiko started to go uphill. She ascended at a clip, noticing how her well-tuned body moved with power and grace. She was as tall as a man, generously endowed with plump, fair flesh. There was no way, she thought, that her depression would triumph over her body and soul. Reaching the hilltop, Keiko looked back at the roofs shining in the spring sun. The misery that had engulfed Keiko started to fade away. She felt relieved, as if a painful stomach ache had subsided. All that remained was a slight dull pain that felt almost ticklish. Then a faint ambition welled up inside her.

"I want to let my flowers bloom, so that they may console life's pains and sorrows. I want, at least, to fill this city with them." Keiko felt her ardor and ambition spread their silver, transparent wings and fly off into the shimmering air above Tokyo.

Keiko had stayed in France for six years at the invitation of

Madam Marais, a couturière. At the request of her compatri-
ots in London, she had crossed over to give flower-arranging
lessons there for a month. Feeling chilly in low-backed evening gowns, she had gone out every night to the theater. At
the Queen's she had seen Shaw's *Saint Joan*. The talk of the
town was how the author had mercilessly ridiculed the Maid
of Orleans in his play. Keiko, however, felt that the Maid's
integrity remained unscathed by the sword that Shaw wielded
with such complacent irony. A woman could understand the
essence of being a woman, she thought. It hardly mattered
what others would say. There was a natural power hidden in
every woman, quite unbeknownst to her, though she may be
an idiot or a peasant. It might explode in a fit of passion, transforming her life as if by miracle. Or it might remain dormant
throughout her life. It would not be at all easy to say which
was happier for her, having this power exposed or hidden.

After returning to Paris, Keiko told Madame Marais about
the play.

"They say that genius can sometimes express far more than
he intends. I think Shaw must be a genius," said Madam Marais, smiling her own beautiful smile, a touch of cynicism in
her otherwise demure manner.

"Fear no more as you walk among others with a red flower
between your lips."

One of Keiko's school friends, a novelist, had composed
this line and had it framed for Keiko when she opened her
studio. Young women who came for lessons called it "the
magic of the red flower." They loved to pose with flowers
between their lips, hands on hips, and prance around the studio, thinking they looked like George Sand on the screen. For
a while this was quite the rage at Keiko's studio, and then was
forgotten.

Keiko stood facing a street full of shops, old and new, lined
up in a row on both sides of the wet, deserted road. She knew
rumors of her visits to Kobuse were rampant along the street.
The studio of one of her business rivals was located here. As
she looked at these shops, their storefronts open as if hungry
for gossip, Keiko felt a new wave of uncertainty. Then she

thought of the "magic of the red flower." She felt she could face her fear so long as she marched down the street with a flower firmly clenched between her front teeth. She must not be without her flowers even for a second. Keiko shook her shoulders and started to march ahead, feeling reassured in the power of her being.

She turned right off a pedestrian street in a modest residential area. Kobuse's house was the second one from the corner. The studio was upstairs, with Japanese-style rooms below. Keiko picked a few overgrown shoots off the hawthorn hedge, then lookd up at a new signboard above the pine gates: "Cheng-chün Studio." The classic title was written in Kobuse's Western-style calligraphy. When Keiko saw the sign, still damp from the rain, she had a premonition that Kobuse was not feeling well again.

Outwardly arrogant and aloof, he was in fact extremely sensitive to the changing trends of the art world. From the time when he and Keiko had been fellow students, he had tried every avant-garde style known in Japan. Post-impressionism, Dadaism, expressionism, neo-classicism, surrealism, he had experimented with them all in defiance of popular taste.

Keiko admired Kobuse's youthful combativeness. She was, however, worried that his restless energy would not give him time to dig deeper into what he really wanted out of himself. His paintings assaulted the viewers with derisive brush strokes and dark tones, hinting at the self-doubt and loathing he felt at being a show-off. Puzzled, the critics promptly assigned him to the category "promising young artist." Naturally his paintings did not sell.

Keiko had noticed Kobuse's mounting frustration upon learning that he was suffering from pulmonary tuberculosis.

"So long as I can earn enough, I'll provide for you. You shouldn't fret. It's not good for your health," Keiko told him repeatedly.

"It's not money I'm worried about," said Kobuse. "It's just that a man has to keep proving to the world that he exists."

Abandoning the abstract and putting away his oils, Kobuse had turned to a nostalgic trend for East Asian art and started to paint with ink and brush. Lately Keiko had often heard him mention the names of unfamiliar Chinese masters. She had not realized that Kobuse was desperate enough to rename his studio after one of them and put out a new sign. His illness seemed to transform his already excessive devotion to fashion into an obsession.

In one of the downstairs rooms Keiko found him in bed, a Momoyama-style screen around him. There was quite a mess by his pillow; enameled pots, plates, an ink box, Chinese paper and calligraphy brush lay scattered about.

"What's going on here? Where's the maid?"

Although Kobuse had heard her come in, he had not taken his eyes off an album of picture postcards. Only after Keiko spoke, did he blink and look up at her. An excitable man, he had a high forehead and bushy brows. His narrow, gentle eyes were inflamed, and Keiko recognized a touch of fear in them. His naturally pallid face now looked absolutely sallow.

"Shige quit and took off yesterday," he said. "These days a sick bachelor can't keep a maid just on regular pay. You have to marry her and promise to leave everything in her name."

Kobuse sounded sarcastic, then turned serious. "Well, it doesn't really matter. The last couple of days I've been too tired from housework to read or paint. So I've been lying here thinking about you. Without doubt, you're a woman, and you women are blessed with an innate virtue that sees you through most things. What do you think?" Kobuse turned over the pages of the album as if in evidence of his argument. He looked at Keiko with so much affection that she was taken aback. He had never looked at her like this. This time it was Keiko who blinked.

"Nonsense. It's not me we're concerned about. How are you feeling today?" But she wanted to hear more of what he had been thinking. "And why did you drag out that album now?"

It was a thick album that contained a collection of postcards that Keiko had regularly sent to Kobuse from abroad. It was an old and forgotten relic from their shared past.

"As I look at these postcards again," said Kobuse, "I see that you were trying to educate me. You may have bought them just because you liked the landscapes, pictures of plays, paintings, ceramics, or dolls on them. But when you sent them back to me, you always sent the same message along with them. There must be a good three hundred of them, all with different greetings, reports and so on. The interesting thing is that they contain one central idea, and one only."

"And what idea could that be?"

"I think you were quite unaware of it yourself. It goes something like this: 'Under any circumstance I will paint only with real flowers. Paint alone will not do.' Do you remember an incident when I was twenty and you were twenty-two or so? I criticized the picture you painted, the one you did from imagination. You brooded over it for a few days, and then all of a sudden you went to the teacher and told him that you wanted to paint with real flowers. Paint would not do, you said. And you never painted again."

Keiko remembered the incident clearly, and the circumstances surrounding it. Kobuse and she were beginning to fall in love then, and yet the relationship did not go any further. Was it because of the incident that they remained just friends? Keiko had gone home to her father, the head of a school in flower arrangement, and devoted herself to that art instead. And now Kobuse, pushing the album toward her, told her that her youthful assertiveness showed in all the cards she had sent him.

"I certainly wasn't aware of it when I sent you these."

"See for yourself then. Listen, here's a bit of modernist theory of art and then: 'This theory can be applied to my art of flower arrangement. I must express the whole of my soul in my flowers, all my ideas, emotions, everything.' See? I think it's obvious."

Listening to Kobuse, Keiko remembered her vision on the hilltop of silver, transparent wings spread against the Tokyo sky. Was it possible that similar ambitions and emotions had been expressed in those postcards she sent to Kobuse? Under Kobuse's open scrutiny, she felt a bit embarrassed about her earlier vision. All the same she started to fight back a little.

"I see nothing at all strange with what I wrote then. Do you?"

"No, that's my point," said Kobuse, growing more excited. "Everything is clearer now that I've gone back to being an Oriental again. Here's how I see you now. When you were upset at what I said about your painting, you went back home to the family business. That's how you came to devote your life to flowers. Imagine what would have happened if, instead of flower arrangement, a man happened to catch your fancy at that point in your life. I bet you would have given him what you gave your flowers—your body and soul. You would have made him a good wife." Keiko was about to protest, but he stopped her. "That's the sort of woman you are."

There was a morbid power in Kobuse's willful words that made Keiko fall silent. She wondered what Kobuse was trying to achieve by passing judgement on her. It might be that for a sick, excitable man an independent woman appeared much too oppressive. Kobuse might be trying to gain his peace of mind by passing judgement on her, as if she were his subordinate. If that was the case, Keiko had better attend to the question of his health.

"You haven't told me how you're feeling today."

"Not good. Now my digestive system's affected. I'm a lucky guy."

Kobuse's strained and flippant tone when he talked of his health depressed Keiko. She pitied the long-suffering man whose desperate irony was aimed at himself. Yet she could offer him no words of comfort, because she knew he did not wish even to hear them. Having grown tired of his own illness, Kobuse habitually resorted to irony with people like Keiko.

A little chilly, Keiko pulled her kimono sleeves over her hands and looked out at the garden. All the flower beds were gone, and instead a few rocks and bamboos had been placed among hastily patched moss. Busy with her teaching for the last couple of weeks, she had sent Senko to look after Kobuse from time to time. Senko, however, had not mentioned any changes in the garden.

"When did you do it over? Senko didn't tell me."

"Oh, about ten days ago. I know for sure now that I won't be around much longer. So I called in gardeners and had them make it over in only three days. Nobody else but you is to see it. I want it all to myself till I die."

The evening sun cast its rays into the garden over the neighboring roof and fence. The bamboos and rocks turned crimson on one side, shadowy on the other. Wind rustled through the bamboo leaves.

"Isn't it strange that even new bamboo rustles in the wind like it's been there for a long time? When I listen to that sound at night alone, I feel as if all the crazy struggle of the last seventeen, eighteen years seems to be resolved. I also pity myself a bit at times, but not very much."

In the darkening shadows of evening the garden took on a mysterious hue.

"I've come to believe," Kobuse went on, "that the Eastern style best fits the man in the end. It has the perfect light, dry touch."

Keiko felt confused, not knowing how to collect her agitated thoughts. Silently she turned on the light, cleaned a few plates off the floor, and stuck the bundle of money she brought under Kobuse's pillow.

"I'll send Senko over to look after you. You should get a second doctor's opinion. Please don't give up on your life so easily."

As she went out of the room, she looked back at Kobuse's big, handsome body lying exhausted on his sick bed, and wiped her eyes.

An exhibition to celebrate the fifth anniversary of the opening of Keiko's studio was scheduled to take place soon at the height of the cherry blossom season. Keiko was frantically busy, soliciting exhibits from colleagues, making rounds of her sponsors, and trying to prepare all the exhibits planned by her and her students.

With only ten days left before the opening, a problem arose concerning the rental agreement with the hall reserved for the show. Possibly under pressure from Keiko's rival factions, the manager of the hall declined, stating that an exhibit of flower arrangement had never before been shown at the renowned hall. His intermediary explained further that the hall's management was afraid to compromise their reputation if they were to permit an experimental venture by an ambitious newcomer.

The fifth anniversary exhibit was in fact to be Keiko's debut as one of the bright stars at the forefront of flower arrangement. She had hoped to show the effects of modernist techniques, which would defy more traditional ways. For this purpose Keiko had planned to make original uses of rare tropical and arctic plants, dried branches and leaves, as well as such familiar Western flowers as amaryllis, tulips, carnations and dahlias.

Although in high spirits during the preparation of the show, Keiko felt crushed and humiliated when the lease of the gallery fell through in the end. Exhausted, she took to sleeping during the daytime.

The cherry blossoms had faded before Keiko had time to notice. She felt the time racing by faster than her own fretful thoughts. When she locked herself up in the little tea room and laid her head down on a pillow made of woven bamboo, she felt a bit more like her old self. Since sending Senko away to Kobuse's house, Keiko's daily routine had been disturbed. Another apprentice named Kuwako had taken over Senko's chores, but this young woman from California was often too business-like for Keiko's taste. Some chores Keiko felt she had to do herself. There was, for instance, the chamber pot Keiko kept hidden in her bedroom cabinet. Although it was a lovely piece decorated with Persian motifs, cleaning it was one job that Keiko felt no one but herself or her niece should manage.

Kuwako had her merits, however. Keiko was sometimes charmed by her unfamiliarity with Japanese custom. Teachers of flower arrangement often received gifts from students. One day a gift was sent from a downtown restaurant, bonito prepared in the Tosa fashion, on a beautiful Shonzui-style plate. It had been broiled on one side only, the opaque shade of the

cooked side changing into the translucent pink of the raw side.
Staring hard at this unfamiliar dish, Kuwako said to Keiko:
"Looks spoiled to me. Are you sure it's all right?" At such
times Keiko felt Kuwako was as dear as a little boy. She would
hold Kuwako's hand and tell her that it was indeed all right.

Another example of Kuwako's over-zealousness was the
thorough cleaning of the aquarium. The deep green water full
of algae had been replaced with fresh clear water. Keiko was
amused, thinking the change was probably for the better as the
summer approached. The late spring sun filled the deck and
garden with abundant light. It illuminated the aquarium from
one side, transforming it into a crystal vessel for the goldfish
and pebbles inside. The pair of calicos swam around happily in
the clear water, though somewhat puzzled by the brightness.
Their white fan tails and bright spots of color on their bodies
were flowers and trailing plumes in the water. The zebra with
amber eyes stood there as always, its nose against the tank.
The vase on the lid now held a sheaf of green barley.

Keiko gazed at the deck and garden from where she lay,
savoring the quiet interval she finally had time to enjoy again.
Suspended between sleep and wakefulness in a mixture of excitement and worry, Keiko braced herself for yet more trouble
ahead. The thought somehow revived her, and made her look
eagerly to the challenge. What was it with her, she asked herself, so looking forward to a good fight? As her lids became
heavy and her eyes started to close, Keiko's mind, still alert,
would catch a powerful vision of the flowers glowing incan-
descently in the garden.

There was a graceful pond with feminine lines in the garden,
a miniature copied from the Enshu-style garden at the Koku-
bunniji Temple in Yamato. Behind it were cherry trees; in the
foreground, just below the deck, was a large flower bed. Students and florists who came to Keiko's studio often brought
bare-root plants and hothouse flowers past their prime and
added to the bed. Throughout the year it was a profusion of
flowers in and out of season. Her students called it "the nurs-
ing home" or "the group home" for flowers. Now at the end
of spring the blossoms had reached their peak.

As she drifted in and out of her dreamy state, Keiko saw flowers trembling and mingling in a rainbow of colors—Oriental poppies, lupins, dodders, azaleas, asters, sweet peas, irises, lilies of the valley, snapdragons, anemones, hyacinths, roses, Scotch brooms, tulips, California poppies, Shasta daisies, cactus blooms, pinks, petunias, etc. These flowers merged into one gigantic bloom. And the numerous leaves and stems joined to support the giant flower.

A powerful voice came booming: "Om! Om!"

Drops of gleaming dew fell from the giant bloom to the ground. The earth became suddenly transparent, as if in animation, revealing a mass of branching roots. Another booming voice resounded from there: "Om! Om!"

In her dreamy state Keiko wondered if the giant bloom represented an abbey consecrated to Jules Romain's *unanimisme*, which purported a complete systematization of human mystery.

Or perhaps it was a symbol of the poetic catholicism of Paul Claudel, who had so fearlessly proclaimed: "The Lord is in our railway stations and in our theaters."

There were many more questions, other possibilities. In her life as an artist several ideas had touched and moved Keiko profoundly, had taken her breath away and as swiftly left her. No matter how intense they had been, all had had the soft, velvet touch of femininity. All now came back to Keiko in her dream.

The giant flower gave answer to none of her questions. It simply kept booming "Om! Om!" and shook off gleaming drops of dew.

Possibly flowers preceded ideas, the sole origin of beauty without beginning or end, rooted in immediate sensations. Being its own cause and effect, its beauty remained uncompromised. Was it then a great force on earth?

A refined fragrance reached her, fresh and yet subdued. As she began to awaken, Keiko recognized the scent of burnt peony stalks from the studio, where her students were taught to scorch stems and so help flowers absorb water. Quietly, she became alert. The giant flower in her dream slowly separated into individual ones, and they returned to their places in the flower bed.

Keiko found Senko standing absently in the garden.

"Is anything the matter?"

Senko made a shy, formal bow, as if to a stranger. The extreme care she took with her kimono also made her look unfamiliar. What surprised Keiko most, however, was the hint of pride and resolution in Senko's languid face. Having many young girls as students and herself leading a chaste life dedicated to flowers for the last sixteen years, Keiko was more perceptive than most in matters of sex. Immediately she saw that Senko had now become independent, beyond anyone's control. A rift had appeared in the relationship between the single aunt and her young niece, who until then had had no secrets from each other. And who was Senko's lover?

Of course! The answer was a brand against her heart.

"Senko, won't you come in?"

"I'm just running a little errand for Mr. Kobuse." Senko had enough pluck to utter the name out loud with feigned indifference. It was Keiko who acted rather embarrassed.

"Well, have a seat." Keiko placed a cushion by the aquarium, wondering why she was acting as formally as her niece.

Senko told her that Kobuse was not doing well. Although radiation treatment was his only hope, he refused to be admitted to a clinic. At dawn every morning the pain in his abdomen grew worse.

"Whenever he is in pain, he laughs and cries, saying that he'll die after he's had some tea. You can't imagine how worried I get. But he looks so strong. I can't believe it will happen."

Even more than the words, the ardor and devotion so evident in Senko's resolve to save her lover from death was a hard blow to Keiko. Looking back now over her own relationship with Kobuse, which she had denied was love, there was one thing Keiko felt a bit ashamed of, namely the comfort she took from the smell of his body. Kobuse's unusually large though consumptive body gave off a scent as soft as flannel and as sweet as hay. The mere thought of it could soften Keiko's heart even when Kobuse was far away. Its calming effect transcended time and space. It had come to her when she was on the other side of the world from him, approaching the United States by ship on her way back from Europe. One whiff of the scent and Keiko slept soundly in her cabin.

"I can't help it. It's not at all like touching him for real," Keiko would tell herself, rationalizing that her pledge to devote herself only to flowers was still intact.

And now what had happened? Everything was in disarray because this man with whom she supposedly had not been in love was taken, his body scent and all, by another woman. Painful flames raged inside Keiko, devouring her inner repose, good judgement, and dedication to art.

Keiko knew very well that she could reprove neither Kobuse nor Senko. Kobuse was not her lover; she only provided material support. He was free to fall in love with another woman and marry her. The niece did not steal him from her aunt. It was only Senko's sense of propriety that stopped her from announcing this new relationship to her aunt.

"Is there anything he wants to see me about?" asked Keiko, desperately trying to appear calm.

"Nothing in particular. Oh, yes, he said to make sure and get some green tea if you had any good tea around. He's very fond of tea lately."

Keiko found a box of green tea and handed it to Senko along with some money for expenses. Senko took her leave, looking for all the world like a young, newlywed wife.

"Hurry and tell me before Senko comes back. I don't want her to hear." They were in Kobuse's sickroom. Keiko had found time in her busy schedule for this visit. She had chosen the hour carefully, knowing that Senko would go out to the public bath late at night. The secrecy made her feel miserable, but she could not help herself.

"My head isn't what it used to be," said Kobuse, "and I don't care much about anything anymore. What good will it do now?" Holding on to his pillow, he turned over with difficulty. "I guess I can tell you, as long as you ask. We were in love, you and I." He spoke calmly, as if he was talking about someone else.

"I've realized that too, all of a sudden. Still, in all these years I never once thought of marrying you," said Keiko, trying to match Kobuse's detached tone.

"We are a strange pair," Kobuse went on. "You're like a river, wide and straight, flowing on and on, taking up everything that comes your way. It's as if all this had been arranged for you before you were born. And me, I'm more like a pond without much water to begin with. I've managed to waste what I have in a rather short time."

Between sips of tea, Kobuse talked in a hoarse voice, as if his life itself were withering away. He said he did not know whether he had been shrewd or stupid. He had loved Keiko from the beginning, but had not even tried to fight against the powerful current of her life. Listening to the unceasing flow of that ever widening river made him uneasy, especially so for one who knew his own meager supply.

"I remember your very first oil, a picture of peonies. When I saw it I was startled by something strange lurking under its surface, something you wouldn't see in any ordinary picture. I saw an intense ambition spreading its wings and flying up from the canvas. That's why I shouted at you. I said it wasn't a proper painting at all."

"I remember. They were white peonies, pale yet burning."

Kobuse had not been sure whether Keiko had any future in painting or should search a different outlet for her artistic talent. Before thinking that far, he had instinctively rejected her work.

"I just couldn't act otherwise. There are times when a deed is done before any emotion or reason has its say."

While the affair with Senko had marked a clear line between his life and Keiko's, the parting had brought him sorrow as well as relief.

"A vigorous life," said Kobuse, "is a bully against a weaker one. It's got to poke at the other and look it over, not out of hate but fondness. Just like a child examining a baby turtle, making it swim, crawl and roll over, it can't figure out why the other's so much smaller." He had been shocked and confused by the post cards Keiko had so energetically sent him from Europe. In them she introduced and commented on new styles of painting, trying them on and taking them off like fashionable clothes. Kobuse took new ideas more seriously, trying hard to alter himself to fit each new fad. But it merely hastened the work of exhausting his life supply.

"That's not true, not true at all." Keiko put a hand to the quilt he had half thrown off. "I just wanted to see you become an original artist. That's all. I wasn't bullying or poking fun at all."

Kobuse showed signs of fatigue. "No, it's the truth. And it was a disguised expression of love on your part. You see, love between the vigorous and the weak can only turn out to be tragic."

Keiko thought she understood. The realization, however, that their relationship had come to an end hit her hard. She broke down and cried.

"But I'm not as strong as you think I am. What am I to live for now?"

Kobuse took a deep breath and sat up on his bed. Stroking her ample back, he said: "Come, now. You're a big girl, thirty-eight years old, and such a pretty one too. It may be hard for a while, I know, but you'll get over it."

Keiko felt this was the time to say what must be said: "Was it to hurt me that you took up with Senko?"

"No." He stopped his hand for a moment, then began to stroke her back again. "No, it was more like submitting to the will of nature, I suppose. You see, nature has to leave at least a child behind for a man who's never completed anything else."

Exhausted, he lay down again. He straightened his back a little, and, with his hands on his forehead, he said to no one in particular: "Maybe by the time the child is grown up, medicine will have made enough progress that tuberculosis won't be so deadly."

Keiko spent the whole year in lethargy over the failure to rent the gallery and Kobuse's affair. Ironically, however,

Keiko's fame and reputation grew so much during this period that the gallery was actually asking to hold her next exhibition.

This welcome turn of events did not move her as it would once have. Accomplishments, she had always felt, were an end, not a beginning. What she needed was a push to bring her out of her gloom and make a fresh start.

"Fear no more as you walk among others with a red flower between your lips."

Once again Keiko relied on the line her friend had inscribed for her. She would bite hard on that flower and hold onto it with all her power. By so doing, extraordinary strength and vision would come to her to pull her out of her inertia. And she was not mistaken.

The principles governing Keiko's love and understanding of flowers can be summed up as follows:

The colors of flowers originate directly from their life force. They are purer than any artificial paint, and it was with such colors that Keiko wished to paint her pictures. In man-made paints there are opposites that clash and repel each other. Not so the colors of flowers, which are brought out by the rays of the sun. Each color is unique and indivisible, no matter how mixed in color it may seem. A combination of pure colors does not suffer from conflict or disharmony. For this reason a flower can hold its own all by itself or in mass.

The form of a flower is the idea of the universe, encompassing all. In the world of flowers even reproductive organs become grand and noble. Upon reading *Le Chef-d'oeuvre Inconnu* by Balzac, Keiko had wept over the failure of its hero, a painter who, in seeking the perfection of his art, covered his canvas with mad, incomprehensible objects. What a pleasure it would be, she had thought, to show such a man the world of flowers.

What a delicate and secret pleasure they gave, the flowers one would touch upon waking in the night! Flowers had a way of stimulating the glands and stirring one artistically. (Did she feel so young because of this? Keiko would wonder.)

A few more observations on flowers will suffice. One of the

Buddhist sutras explains the flower as "the cosmic symbol of the perfect being who blooms forth from an ideal seed that is nurtured by enduring all that is hard and difficult in human life." It also says: "To love flowers is like an unenlightened being longing for supreme wisdom." Keiko herself has said: "Even the tiniest of flowers expresses the life and character of all of its kind. How vigorous is the force that enables a flower to bloom under the sun, transforming all earthly filth into nutrients for itself. Mighty is the flower."

And so, at length, the day for the opening of Keiko's floral pageant arrived. Her paintings in flowers filled all the rooms on all the floors of the exhibition hall.

The major pieces were as follows:

The First Floor: In the foyer stood a huge lacquered vessel shaped like a boat, containing a massive pine trunk with wisteria hanging from the branches. A fireplace made of mahogany, light brass and gray marble gave a shimmering, ethereal impression. A lone spray of red quince was on the mantlepiece. A sake bucket made of wood grained like fish scales and copper hoops sat by the window. A pair of vines grew out of the bucket and crept up the window frame, forming a dark green shadow. In it red berries and small flowers shone like rubies wrapped in silk. At one corner of the room stood a winding bridge made of a gloomy leaden material, arranged in the Yatsuhashi pattern. It was surrounded by irises, as if to make one think of a passionate scene from the courtly past.

The Second Floor: At the head of the stairway to the right sat an unglazed pottery as big as a little knoll. An enormous red camelia, at least several decades old, stood in it. To its left a big rattan cage contained not singing birds but tricolored flowers from the South Seas. A diamond-shaped lantern held a lavender light of lilacs behind a pillar. A box protruding from the wall contained a trim metallic vase with a few stalks of dried reeds and three calla lilies, like a saint with his faithfuls. The front of the room was a huge flower bed with a great, sunny mass of peonies, and white light behind it like the rising moon.

The Third Floor: The big alcove of the black-lacquered study held a statue of the Kudara Kannon raising its hand in a magical gesture that would dispell all fears. The upraised hand of the statue was balanced by the hemp flowers in a vase shaped like a ceremonial vessel from ancient China. Behind them hung a scroll of summerscape by Sesson. In the side alcove there was a sophisticated, eight-petaled vase with red and yellow roses, evoking the opulence of the Rokumeikan days.

The Tea Cottage: There was a spray of colza half gone to seed in an old oil urn in the small alcove. The scroll was a drawing of orchids by Hachidai-sanjin.

A Corner of the Hallway: A large porcelain basin held a confused mass of white and red carnations. "Battle Scene" was its title.

The Dining Room: Rhododendrons and tiger lilies were arranged in a cermaic mug from the Hofbrauhaus in Munich. A small two-handled vase held a spray of maguerite and sweet pea. Hornwort and water lilies swam in a big saucer of Venetian glass.

Each arrangement had a name: The Unai Maiden of Ashiya, Harp, Song, Faust's Reverie, A Silent Repose, Gray Hair, Renaissance, Pastoral, George Sand, Ancient Capitol, Gothic, Lady Murasaki, First Love, Banquet, Rhyme, and many more.

Then there was a special room, a very large one. It contained two of Keiko's arrangements that attracted particular attention during the exhibit. Set somewhat apart from works by her students, one was called "Cradle," the other "Coffin." The lovely cradle was woven of iron and synthetic fibers and held a single tulip bulb. At first sight the arrangement seemed too simple, yet it created the most graceful and refreshing effect. The large coffin was a slab of Chichibu serpentine with a man-shaped opening in the middle. Inside an arrangement of lillies of the valley rested peacefully.

At the exhibit Keiko was wearing a dress of the palest shade of blue that did not clash with any flowers, whichever arrangement she chose to stand beside. Always smiling, she mingled with the crowd that gathered from all over the city, bowing and thanking her acquaintances as they offered their congratulations. She also bowed to newspaper reporters who promised favorable reviews of these bold and innovative works.

Then it was night and the hall was deserted. Senko, who had come in a car to bring Keiko home, had worn herself out going through the exhibit with her baby. She had gone to the dining room for something to drink. Keiko went up alone to the roof garden and stood beneath the dark sky.

"Kobuse." Keiko cried, holding a handkerchief to her eyes.

"Kobuse." Although it was his name she called, her tears were shed more for herself, for her life full of strange ironies, sharp pains and hidden passion.

Then, suddenly, she knew. All the flowers in the building below were supporting her in union. Like a breath of eternal freshness, they were the bold strength lending support to her life. They were her life itself.

"Mighty is the flower."

No longer weeping, she nodded firmly. As the night breeze gently shook the hem of her dress, Keiko stood there in the dark, herself one big flower.

Original title: *Hana wa Tsuyoshi* (1937).

About the Editor and Translators:

Yukiko Tanaka, Ph.D., was born in Yokohama, Japan. She came to live in the United States in 1969, where she earned her doctorate in comparative literature from the University of California, Los Angeles. She co-edited and co-translated the anthology *This Kind of Woman: Ten Stories by Japanese Women Writers, 1960-1976* (Stanford University Press, 1982) and is currently working on a history of Japanese women writers from the beginning of the modern era through World War II. Dr. Tanaka has also translated a number of stories for various journals and anthologies, most recently "Iron Fish" by Kono Taeko in *Shōwa Anthology: Modern Japanese Short Stories* (Tokyo: Kodansha International, 1986).

Elizabeth Hanson has degrees in both journalism and Japanese studies and lived for several years in Japan. She has published articles, essays, poetry and short fiction, and is also co-translator and co-editor of *This Kind of Woman: Ten Stories by Japanese Women Writers, 1960-1976*.

Hiroko Morita Malatesta holds a Ph.D. in Oriental Languages from the University of California, Los Angeles. She has taught Japanese language, literature and culture at a number of universities, and her articles in English and Japanese have appeared in several academic journals.

WOMEN IN TRANSLATION
Explore the World of International Women's Writing

The translation series is printed on acid-free paper and also available in cloth editions. For further information please write to The Seal Press, 3131 Western Avenue, #410, Seattle, Washington 98121-1028.